High
Performance
Recruiting

High
Performance
Recruiting

A Practical Guide to
Becoming a Valued Business Partner

Stacy Rogers

iUniverse, Inc.
New York Lincoln Shanghai

High Performance Recruiting
A Practical Guide to Becoming a Valued Business Partner

iUniverse books may be ordered through booksellers or by contacting:

iUniverse
2021 Pine Lake Road, Suite 100
Lincoln, NE 68512
www.iuniverse.com
1-800-Authors (1-800-288-4677)

To contact the author, please send email to: careerstrategies@windstream.net

ISBN-13: 978-0-595-42781-9 (pbk)
ISBN-13: 978-0-595-87113-1 (ebk)
ISBN-10: 0-595-42781-2 (pbk)
ISBN-10: 0-595-87113-5 (ebk)

Printed in the United States of America

Contents

PREFACE

I began my recruiting career during the dot.com days, getting my feet wet in IT contract and contingency placements. I later worked for "Corporate America" where I learned more about healthcare and executive recruiting, as well as learning how to develop and lead a staffing program. Now as a human resources instructor and consultant I've hired, trained and mentored recruiters at various professional levels. Over the years, I've often been asked what it takes to be a successful recruiter. I simply answer that it first takes a desire to succeed and continually learn. While these are keys to success, they're only the tip of the iceberg.

If you were to review an ad for a recruiter twenty years ago, you would probably see responsibilities similar to "place ads", "screen resumes", "schedule interviews" and "send offer letters". Notice anything about these? They're all administrative tasks. Technically, administration wasn't the theme for all recruiters. Third party recruiting has always been focused on sales and the bottom line. However, these recruiters often focused on placement volume. These days, volume and administration will not get it done. Recruiting success and performance are measured by different gauges and by higher standards. You now see recruiting positions that emphasize strategy, quality and developing business partnerships. This is an exciting and challenging transformation for recruiters!

To revisit the question concerning successful recruiting ... well, this question is why I decided to write this book. The information found here attempts to answer this based largely upon my own professional development and experience. The book is structured according to the approach I use when mentoring and coaching recruiters. It is a simple and practical guide that provides helpful practices, tips, and forms that you may readily apply.

Before beginning, it is important to note that not every organization is alike. Some will require different competencies and responsibilities may vary.

Policies, processes and cultures differ from one employer to another. And as we speak, organizations are changing! Therefore, some information in the book is based upon generalizations—what *I've* found to be common or typical. It is not intended to be the "bible" of what occurs for every case, organization, environment, market or region. Therefore, it is recommended that you conduct further research for specific recruiting positions, companies and markets.

This book is written for recruiters wanting to become valued business partners. It's also for anyone new to, or just interested in, the recruiting profession. Lastly, it's for my students because I know how difficult it is to comprehend and apply information from texts.

CHAPTER ONE

Introduction to Recruiting

What is High Performance Recruiting?

On the surface, some may contend that high performance recruiting simply refers to those recruiters capable of filling positions fast. This is a common misconception and couldn't be further from the truth! **There are expected operating and quality levels with anything dubbed as "high performance" so there's more to it than just high output (volume).** Then what exactly does high performance recruiting mean? What differentiates high performance recruiters from other recruiters? Let's begin by building this framework.

Webster's Dictionary defines "recruit" as follows:

> "To enlist (new members) for an organization" (Agnes, 2003, p. 539).

Of course, you may recruit individuals for the military, memberships and so on but in this context, we'll be focusing on employment. We'll also be focusing on strategic recruiting as opposed to administration. Therefore, the context of this book will be based on the following description of recruiting:

> Recruiting is a competitive process of acquiring and deploying talent within the workforce and is strategically aligned with the organization's business needs and goals.

High performance recruiters do this well. In fact, they do it so well that they are sought after by other companies. They are the A players of their field and are valuable assets to ANY organization in ANY environment because they know how to adapt and exceed expectations. **They understand the importance of setting and meeting goals. They develop and execute their strategy. They manage relationships with both candidates and hiring managers. They continuously improve and are always proactive.**

High performance recruiting doesn't require an open position in order to begin. In fact, it hinges on being proactive in every aspect of the recruitment lifecycle (discussed in the next chapter). Therefore, high performance recruiters will proactively source and screen candidates and market their "stars" to hiring managers. They find or create openings before the requisitions come down the pike. When requisitions are received, they have an active pool of talented candidates in which they readily refer to for the position(s) or for referrals. Sound familiar to sales and marketing? If it does, that's because it is!

Recruiting is the only profession **responsible for bringing two distinct parties at opposite ends of the spectrum through the sales process to come together and "buy into" a mutually beneficial relationship.** Most sales people sell distinct products or services directly to a client, which is one-dimensional. Recruiters must sell a position, compensation, work climate and manager to the candidate. Conversely, they must also sell the candidate's individual talents and potential bottom line contributions to the hiring manager. **Whether recruiters are directly working with a client, an account manager or a hiring manager within their own company, they must always sell to two distinct parties!** By comparison, this is then two-dimensional, as shown in figure 1.1. In cases where the recruiter is a third party (e.g., a search firm recruiter), he/she must seek a win-win situation for all three parties (the client, candidate and his/her employer). What a unique dynamic!

Figure 1.1

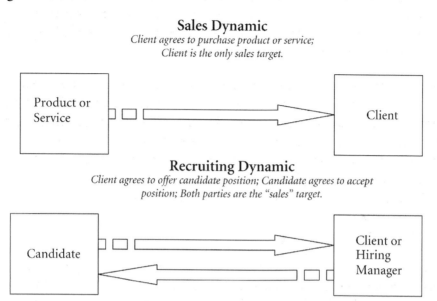

Sales Dynamic
Client agrees to purchase product or service;
Client is the only sales target.

Recruiting Dynamic
Client agrees to offer candidate position; Candidate agrees to accept
position; Both parties are the "sales" target.

Search and professional staffing firms (third parties) most often seek recruiters with sales mentalities. These recruiters are usually compensated in the same fashion with commissions and/or incentives. They are charged with finding the best candidates for their clients through various means that include proactive sourcing tactics. These tactics may include networking, referrals, cold calling and professional lists, among others. **They can not afford to wait and hope that the right candidates will come to them. They must find top talent before their competition does!** This is best compared to the way colleges/universities recruit athletes. Scouts (recruiters) seek out the best players, evaluate their statistics, observe their games, reach out to the prospect and discuss the benefits of playing for their college or university. In other words, these scouts find the players before the players find them. Scouts not only seek out the talented players, but establish relationships with them. They may meet with potential players and their families, keep in touch by phone or letters, send information and provide tours of the campus. In cases of highly touted players, scouts are often competing with many other colleges/universities. This is similar to the competition that recruiters face when seeking to hire top talent.

In corporate (internal) environments, however, recruiting was historically viewed as more of an administrative function. Recruiters were often charged with posting ads in the paper, filtering resumes to hiring managers and ensuring applicants filled out the appropriate paperwork. With this, came a reactive mentality of sourcing candidates. Waiting for a position to open, posting an ad in the newspaper, then waiting for candidates to apply was generally the norm. This was how the role was defined which set the tone for a "let's see if we get lucky" attitude. This is one of the main reasons why many professional positions were outsourced to third party recruiters. For these reasons, internal recruiters seldom played a key strategic role in hiring their own company's talent. These days will soon be long gone and **the administrative recruiter will be a thing of the past**, at least for those companies that wish to remain competitive.

In recent years, organizations have realized that their internal recruiters must be more proactive when finding, attracting and building relationships with top talent. The people that recruiters hire, collectively known as the workforce, are the ones that perform the duties responsible for making a company successful (or not successful). Therefore, **the link is easily made between recruiting and the company's bottom line.** In these days of "human capital management", "the war for talent" and "A players vs. C players," recruiting has been brought to the forefront and viewed as a function just as important (or almost as important) as operations, sales and finance. Because of this, **internal recruiters must have or develop competencies in planning, strategy development, relationship management and consultation.**

It is the intent of this book to address professional recruiting at this level. Whether you're planning to become a recruiter or wanting to develop into a high performance recruiter, this book will provide the competencies, processes, best practices and useful tips for a roadmap to success.

Recruiter Competencies

So what does it take to be a *good* professional recruiter? Professional recruiting is a very exciting field. **It is a sales, marketing, project management and human resources role, among others, all rolled into one.** Because of all of these dynamics involved, it takes a well-rounded person to be a *good* recruiter. However, in addition to this, **it takes business acumen, strategy, determination, drive, a** hard work ethic and integrity to be a *high performance* recruiter. And these are just a few of the ingredients!

Mediation is a field that has a similar dynamic to recruiting, although mediation isn't related to sales. While mediation differs from recruiting in many ways, there is a common denominator among these two professions. Mediators must work to bring two parties together for resolution. Recruiters must also seek resolution between two parties (candidate and hiring manager) by negotiating salaries, benefits, accommodations (such as flexible work schedules, equipment, relocation, etc.) and come to an "offer acceptance". Therefore, **recruiters, like mediators, must be very good with interpersonal interactions, conflict resolution, persuasion, negotiations and most of all they must be good listeners—not just for the spoken word(s), but also the unspoken word(s).**

Recruiters must also be project managers and manage candidates as they progress through the recruitment lifecycle (discussed in Chapter Two). Items must be completed before going onto another stage or process while at times, multiple stages or processes are performed in parallel. **So with this comes organization, meeting deadlines, attention to detail and multi-tasking. They must have the ability to prioritize and have multiple activities going on at one time, including multiple positions and candidates!**

Recruiters must have the ability to work individually *and* as a team. At some stages in the recruiting lifecycle, such as sourcing, it requires autonomy and individual judgment. At other stages, it may require teamwork with the client, candidate, support staff, vendors or others. **If a group of recruiters are working together, it's important that each is team oriented by sharing information and keeping an open flow of communication.** This prevents duplication of work, builds team rapport and provides better service to both hiring managers and candidates.

Recruiters must also have business acumen. They must understand business fundamentals, industry dynamics, performance, trends, projections, products and/or service offerings. They must be able to communicate to, and think like, business people. They must align their goals with company goals, develop plans, execute against those plans, make adjustments as needed and measure their performance. In other words, **they must think and perform their craft in terms of how they contribute to the bottom line.**

As do many professions, recruiters often work in demanding, competitive and ever-changing environments requiring them to be **flexible, adaptable and have the ability to work under pressure.** To some, this is exciting and challenging. To others, it may be too much to handle. Not all environments are like this. It is more typical in the third party (external) recruiting environments, although internal environments may also be thwart with demands from hiring managers and pressure to fill positions fast and with quality candidates. High pressure environments may elicit unethical behavior to stay competitive or to land a client or candidate. Don't fall into this trap! **Do what's right and take the high road. Unethical behavior *will* damage your reputation.**

Technology plays a major role in recruiters' lives with regard to the Internet, email, databases, applicant tracking systems and office technology to include word processing programs, presentation software and spreadsheets. So there's no question that **recruiters must be up-to-date with technology.** Other technological advances in recruiting are cell phones, palm pilots and handheld pc's making the recruiter potentially available at all times. Many high performance recruiters do make themselves available at all times to stay ahead of the competition. Working all hours and becoming a "slave" to technology isn't necessarily required to be a high performance recruiter. **However, thinking strategically and using technology to your advantage is required.**

Lastly, **recruiters must provide excellent service to those in which they come in contact.** This includes applicants (those who apply), candidates (those who are qualified and are contacted), hiring managers, co-workers and vendors. Recruiters should be able to effectively manage relationships and provide constructive feedback and prompt follow-up. **Recruiters must also be able to differentiate those applicants they can help from those they can not help.** This is very important because recruiters aren't able to place all applicants that come to them. For example, an executive recruiter will not be able to place someone with just front-line supervisory experience. Such feedback should be handled with care and tact. More than likely, the applicant will appreciate the honesty and any referrals the recruiter is able to provide.

In summation, the following are the knowledge, skills and abilities discussed that a high performance recruiter should possess. Keep in mind that this list is not all inclusive!

- Ability to effectively manage relationships and provide excellent customer service to both clients and candidates
- Excellent oral and written communication skills
- Proficient in developing and executing recruitment strategies that align with company goals
- Proven ability to multi-task and prioritize workflow in a fast-paced environment
- Ability to meet tight deadlines and produce under pressure
- High attention to detail and organization
- Ability to work autonomously and as a team
- Demonstrated high energy, sense of urgency and desire to succeed
- Knowledge of or ability to learn specific business terms and concepts
- Proficient in navigating the internet, office technology, recruitment software and other computer-related programs
- Ability to persuade and negotiate terms with the candidate and/or client throughout the recruitment lifecycle
- High level of integrity and ethical values

Differentiating the Recruiting Environments

As mentioned previously, internal recruiters are becoming increasingly important to C-level executives (e.g., CEO, COO or CFO) and are now considered an important contributing factor to the company's bottom line. This conclusion is drawn from the fact that **recruiters are responsible for hiring the talent within the organization. It is this collective, organizational talent that sets the standard for company performance through leadership, productivity, quality, service and innovation.** Because of the increasing importance now placed on internal recruiters and their ability to attract top talent, companies are seeking higher levels of knowledge, skills and abilities (KSA's) for these roles than they have in the past. While competencies may be leveling amongst the internal and external recruiting roles, the environments are often very different. It is important to distinguish these environments to understand the differences and similarities as we explore high performance recruiting throughout this book.

External recruiting will be discussed in the context of search firms and professional staffing firms (contract services). The Internal environment will be discussed in the context of corporations and consulting firms. Consulting firms share some characteristics with the external environments. Therefore, they may also fall under this category on occasion.

Keep in mind that there are other environments in which recruiting is performed, for example, staffing companies focusing on industrial or clerical placements. There are also research firms that focus on sourcing lists of passive candidates and selling them to their clients (at the request of the client, they may also perform prescreening). There are many industries, such as manufacturing, that don't have a dedicated recruiter, but have an HR Generalist or HR Manager that handles the recruiting efforts. While each of these is viable recruiting environments, this book will focus on recruiters responsible for professional placements through the entire recruitment lifecycle. However, anyone that performs, or wishes to perform, in any recruiting capacity will benefit from this book.

EXTERNAL ENVIRONMENTS

External environments consist of third party recruiters that perform recruiting or staffing services for their clients. Search firms are outsourced to fill their clients' full-time positions. This means that the search firm sources and assists with selecting the candidate, but the client becomes the employer. Professional staffing firms, on the other hand, recruit candidates to perform contract services for their clients. Unlike search firms, professional staffing firms are the employer and manage the employer-employee relationship (payroll, benefits, etc.). Professional staffing firms are considered external because they recruit for specific client openings and the client supervises the work of the contract employee. The following sections will further detail the search and professional staffing firm environments.

Search Firms:

Search firms focus only on full-time placements. This means that their clients hire the selected candidates as full time employees. Some firms focus on placements at or above a specific salary. For example, some professional search firms may not work on positions below $75,000. Other firms may have a specialization. For example, some have a niche in the medical profession. Others may focus on the legal profession, human resources, engineering, information technology or education. For just about every profession, there is probably a search firm that focuses on that industry.

For these placements, search firms may charge a contingency fee when the person is placed or they may require a retainer fee. There are distinct differences in how these two payment plans work. **The contingency fee is a set percentage, usually around 30%, based upon the candidate's initial annual salary.** For instance, if the placement's annual salary is $100,000, the search firm makes $30,000 with a 30% contingency fee arrangement. Therefore, the client doesn't pay until the placement is made. However, the firm may be working with other clients and may not put top priority on one given position or client.

Retained searches usually occur for high level executive positions. These are positions that require the utmost care and attention. Clients pay a retained search firm to work only on their position, often until the position is filled. The disadvantage for the client is that they must continue to pay the firm with no guarantee of a placement. The firm is strictly being paid for services. The advantage for the client is that the firm or recruiter is solely focused on their position and is not distracted with other searches.

Search firm recruiters typically develop and manage their own accounts. Therefore, they perform sales, account management and recruiting roles working very closely with their clients and candidates to find the right match. They may enlist the help of researchers on staff (or sometimes outsourced) to do the sourcing and prescreening, but they may also do this themselves depending upon how large the firm is. **Most candidates contacted by search firm recruiters are passive, meaning they're not actively looking for a position.** Their names may be obtained from referrals, professional lists, subscription lists, networking, internet or industry research or cold calling.

These recruiters are in a very competitive environment as they may be competing with other firms to fill clients' positions. Therefore, they are usually available 24/7 and must be on top of their game. They must be proactive and assertive, constantly pursuing avenues to contact "A players" and obtain new clients. At the same time, they must manage the clients and candidates they currently have. The client trusts them as their advisor and consultant during the search process and recruiters in these firms may also hold the title of "Placement Consultant" or "Recruitment Consultant", among others.

Once search firm recruiters make a placement, they no longer "court" the candidate they placed. They may follow up with their placement to ensure everything is going ok and attempt to prevent any flight risks within the first few weeks or months of employment. This is because there are often guarantees in place that the employee will stay for a certain length of time (usually 90 or 180 days). If the new hire doesn't stay during the guaranteed period, the search firm places someone else free of charge. Sometimes a refund is guaranteed but this is rare. These recruiters may also stay in touch with their placements to solicit referrals or to gain inside information about the client's upcoming openings. **However, search firm recruiters must be careful about soliciting their clients' employees for other positions.** This is bad for business! Clients will quickly drop a firm if they find that the very recruiters that are helping them fill positions are "stealing" their employees.

Recruiters in these firms are often paid commission only or a draw (money paid to them on a regular payroll basis, but deducted from their commission when a placement is made). However, they are sometimes paid a base salary plus commission. Because they are paid for each placement they make, their salaries can be very lucrative (six figures) given they are a high performer. However, compensation may vary depending upon several other factors, including the firm's employment brand and market, among others.

Professional Staffing Firms (Contract Staffing):

Professional staffing firms focus on contract placements ("contract" in this sense simply refers to those placements that have a limited duration). **Staffing firms recruit and hire the professional, meaning they are the employer.** However, the employee works under the direction and supervision of the client. These placements have an end or are "temporary" but may be long

term, in some cases, several years in length. When the assignment ends, the professional is no longer an employee unless he or she is placed on another assignment.

Clients usually need contract professionals due to peak seasons, new business, new projects, leaves of absence or other reasons requiring additional staff. **However, these staffing firms shouldn't be confused with industrial or clerical "temp agencies" because on average, they require more highly skilled professionals.** The pay for these contract employees may be as much as $150 per hour, depending upon the type of person and skills required. There are certain skills in IT, for example, that are extremely hard to come by. Therefore, individuals with such skills have leverage when it comes to pay.

Unlike search firms, most professional staffing firm candidates are active, meaning they are actively seeking positions. There is a percentage of the workforce that prefers contract work and only accepts such assignments to earn their living. They prefer to work with many different companies and on many different projects to diversify their skills/experience and to fulfill their own need for independence. Some may often have to travel to other cities to work and may often take off certain periods of the year to spend with their families. In other words, they choose to be contract employees and usually have no desire to work as a full-time employee.

There are others that may have lost their jobs and are willing to work on contract assignments until they find something more "permanent", or rather, with more stability. This is another group of people that professional staffing firms may target. There are often "contract-to-hire" opportunities where clients want to hire a contractor as a full-time employee after the contract period has ended. There may also be short term projects that these individuals may fill in the interim until they move on to full-time employment.

Another segment of the workforce wants to take on additional work after hours or on the weekends. These individuals often work with professional staffing firms to find such arrangements and may work on ongoing projects or intermittently as needed. As you may see, there are many highly skilled professionals who actively seek employment with professional staffing firms.

Professional staffing firms usually charge their clients an hourly bill rate for their contract employee's services. This rate includes sourcing and selecting the employee, in addition to administering payroll, benefits and managing the employer-employee relationship. Therefore, if the bill rate is $75/hr. for a given contractor, this is the firm's *total revenue* for that placement but it's far from their *gross profit (GP)* margin. The most obvious direct cost for the firm is the contract employee's pay. However, there are additional costs, as outlined below:

- Worker's compensation
- Unemployment insurance
- Employer's social security tax contribution
- Benefits (optional, but often necessary to attract the best employees)

Note: These are calculated in most organizations to determine employment costs and/or the monetary value of all employer-related contributions.

These are usually calculated as fixed cost percentages and are multiplied by the contract employee's pay. For example, payroll fees (items in the first 3 bullets) may cost 10–15%. Depending upon the benefits offered, this may add another 0–20%. Therefore the burden percentage (employment costs other than pay) could be anywhere between 10–35% of the contract employee's pay. Professional staffing firms usually assess their burden each year, determine a fixed percentage and apply this percentage for all placements to determine employment costs. There may be two different burden percentages: one for the employees that are eligible for and select benefits (usually those on long term assignments) and one for those that are not eligible for or don't select benefits. Obviously, the contractors that don't receive benefits have a lower burden percentage.

The pay and burden are then used to determine the gross profit (GP) for each placement. **The GP is calculated by subtracting the pay and burden from the bill rate** as illustrated in the formula below:

GP = Bill Rate – Pay – (Pay x Burden %)

The following example further illustrates how the gross profit is calculated.

GP Example (Contract Employee): A staffing firm bills their client $75/hr. and pays their contract employee $40/hr. for an assignment lasting approximately six months. The contract employee is eligible for and selects benefits. The fixed burden for contract employees receiving benefits is 23%. The GP per hour for this particular placement is calculated as follows:

GP = $75 – $40 – ($40 x .23)

GP = $35 – $9.20 = **$25.80/hr.**

In the example above, the firm stands to make more than $25,000 in gross profit for the entire assignment (given the work weeks are a standard 40 hours). Again, assignments can be a year or longer in length, so these placements can become much more lucrative than direct placements. By comparison, the search firm receives a $24,000 fee (30% contingency) for placing a professional with a similar salary (approximately $80,000/year). However, unlike the search firm, the professional staffing firm doesn't receive a lump sum payment when the candidate is placed. Instead, they're paid in increments (usually billed weekly or bi-weekly as timesheets are received) throughout the assignment. The professional staffing firm, therefore, must be able to pay the contractor prior to receiving their client's payments. It may take up to thirty days (more or less) before the professional staffing firm is paid for their contract employee's services. Also, unlike search firms, professional staffing firms must **manage the employer-employee relationship for the duration of the assignment, requiring more work on their part.** However, they **may place one contractor on many assignments given he or she meets the position requirements and are available to work.** Therefore, a "star contractor" can prove to be very lucrative for the professional staffing firm. Given the previous example, if the staffing firm is able to place a contract employee on three similar assignments (same bill rate, pay and duration) they will make more than $75,000 in GP.

There are instances when contractors prefer to be a 1099 or, in other words, independent consultants. This means that they are not on the firm's payroll and are their own entity for IRS purposes. They usually charge a higher pay rate because they must assume the payroll taxes and fees themselves. **Therefore, their pay rate is the total cost for the firm and no burden is applied** as outlined in the example below:

Independent Consultant GP Example: The client's bill rate is $75/hr. and the independent consultant is paid $50/hr. She sends an invoice for each hour worked, similar to a vendor relationship. The GP is calculated as follows:

GP = $75 – $50 = **$25/hr.**

Notice that while there is no additional payroll or benefits burden for the staffing firm, the GP may level out because of the higher rate.

Keep in mind that gross profit and net profit are not the same. The net is what's left after all expenses have been paid, to include internal salaries, office space, utilities, equipment, advertising, etc.

The competition in this industry is extremely competitive. Clients may be working with several firms to fill one position! Like search firms, these recruiters may make themselves available nights and weekends to avoid losing a star candidate to a competitor. In some cases, they may manage their own client accounts but in other cases, there may be account managers that do this. In the account manager/recruiter model, however, the recruiter may still work with the client in some fashion. They may accompany the account manager during client meetings or visits. They may contact hiring managers directly when it comes to details of the search or to obtain candidate feedback. This allows the recruiter to be more effective in understanding exactly what the client wants and needs. However, in this recruiting model, the level of recruiter/client interaction will ultimately depend upon the firm's policies and culture.

In contract staffing, the recruiter becomes the contract employee's "agent". As noted previously, the recruiter continues to stay in contact with the employee and works to place him or her in future assignments. This is very different than the search firm environment where the recruiting relationship soon ends when the candidate is placed.

Recruiters in these environments are usually paid a base salary plus commission based upon their gross profit. In some firms, a team commission may also be paid to the recruiters to promote teamwork. They're sometimes paid commission only or a draw. Some "senior" recruiters in successful firms may make lucrative salaries, but salary levels vary widely depending upon the recruiter's and firm's performance, market and employment brand, among others.

THE INTERNAL ENVIRONMENT

Internal environments are those in which the recruiters and hiring managers work for the same company. Recruiters in this environment are not a third party and only recruit for their organization's internal positions. Corporate environments with internal recruiters obviously fall under this category. Consulting firms, on the other hand, are a bit tricky. They do have internal recruiters that focus on the firm's full-time positions. At the same time, they recruit employees that perform direct services for external clients. The following sections will further detail the corporate and consulting firm environments.

Corporate environments:

As noted previously, corporate recruiting environments consist of recruiters and hiring managers that work for the same company. **These recruiters are not a third party as are those in external environments.** Most often, corporations have a centralized or decentralized recruiting operation. In a centralized environment, recruiters report to the same person, usually a recruiting director or manager. They usually have "client groups" in which they are accountable. A client group in this sense is simply a department (or group) for which the recruiter is responsible for filling positions. A recruiter may be charged with filling all of the finance and accounting positions, while another is charged with filling positions in sales, while still another focuses on IT.

Conversely, recruiters in decentralized settings don't report to the same person, but each one (or small groups) report to a different manager. This is most often determined by location or functional responsibility. For example, a recruiter may report to the HR Manager for a given location and will focus on all positions for that location rather than a specialty area. At the same time, other decentralized recruiters may very well have a specialty area. For example, a recruiter may report to the operations director and only recruit for these positions.

Recruiters in this environment should have a very good understanding of their business, services, products, etc. to appropriately "market" this information to prospective candidates. They should be knowledgeable of the positions (in general) for which they're recruiting, their respective departments and the culture. This is accomplished by partnering with the hiring managers and those involved in the interviewing process. This is also true of external recruiters. However, **internal recruiters only have one company to sell and should have broader and deeper knowledge of their own company.**

These environments are not typically as competitive as external recruiting environments and recruiters may often be able to work a standard work week. They are not usually on call or taking calls at nights or on weekends unless there's an urgent need to fill a position or a major recruiting campaign is underway. **While corporate recruiters don't necessarily compete with other recruiters or firms as do external recruiters, they do compete for talent. They are seeking to hire top talent that will quickly contribute to the company's bottom line and this is always a challenge, no matter if you're internal or external.**

There are also demands from management to fill positions quickly and with quality people. Recruiters must be able to persuade the hiring manager to allow more time to find the right person but at the same time, work diligently to expedite the recruitment process. Conversely, hiring managers may be too picky and not recognize transferable competencies or the value of other skills. These are insights that a recruiter should uncover and point out to the hiring manager. **A partnership between the recruiter and hiring manager has become crucial and without this partnership, recruiting will likely take longer and be less effective.** Under these circumstances, the company may seek the services of an outside search firm. This is not only an additional cost for the company, but securing outside recruiting services may diminish the value of the internal recruiter, especially if it happens often.

Once corporate recruiters place candidates within their company, they may follow up with the new hire in the short term, but they usually don't maintain consistent contact. Retention in these cases, are usually the direct responsibility of the hiring manager and to a broader extent, human resources. However, corporate recruiters often contribute to retention goals indirectly (discussed in Chapter Nine). A few organizations do charge the staffing department with direct retention activities and initiatives.

Internal recruiters are usually paid a base salary and sometimes a bonus. Bonuses may be based upon individual or team recruiting goals met, company performance, quality of hires, manager satisfaction or any other "success" factors deemed appropriate. Corporate recruiters are seeing upward movement in their base salaries and are seeing more performance based pay (bonuses or incentives based upon their contributions), aligning with their increased competency levels and performance expectations.

Consulting Firms:

Consulting firms are outsourced for their expert advice or services. For example, there are technology firms that implement new ERP (Enterprise Resource Planning) systems for their clients. These may take years to plan, implement, customize and train those that will be administering and using the system. These firms secure such projects and deploy their own resources (consultants) to support them. When projects are large in scale or additional resources are needed, the consulting firm must hire additional staff. The consultants may work onsite with their clients, similar to contract employees working for professional staffing firms. However, **unlike professional staffing firms, the client doesn't supervise the work performed.** Consulting firms may partner with professional staffing firms to supplement their staff with contract employees. In other words, consulting firms may become the professional staffing firm's (or even search firm's) client.

Because consultants are full-time employees, they're compensated for "bench time". This simply means that the firm still pays them if they're not actively working on a client project. Consulting firms often provide training during this time or they assign the consultant some internal tasks until redeployed. Being on the bench costs the firm money and the consultant may potentially be laid off due to a lack of work if another project isn't secured in a timely manner.

Consulting firms are paid by the project or by the hour depending upon the client and work involved. Account managers (or other similar title) work directly with clients in an effort to secure entire projects (contracts or service agreements). Once a project is awarded and the contract is signed, the required resources are the firm's responsibility and are not directly determined or chosen by the client. **The recruiter, therefore, works with the firms' project or**

account manager to fill the needed positions. As mentioned, these consultants are full time employees (usually making an annual salary) so the firm must budget their resources and develop compensation levels they may pay in order to make the desired profit.

Because consulting firm recruiters fill their own internal positions, there isn't external competition (other firms competing to fill the same positions). However, they may have significant internal pressure. The firm must retain the project by delivering agreed upon services to the satisfaction of the client (per the contract). If not, the client may wish to seek the services of other firms. Therefore, recruiters may experience internal pressure from firm executives, project managers and/or account managers to acquire and deploy the needed talent.

Like professional staffing firm recruiters, recruiters in this environment are sometimes the consultants' HR contacts. They may also assist with retention programs and workforce planning efforts (determining talent demand and supply, discussed in Chapter Three). Because of this, they may keep close contact with the consultants they hire. This is more typical for smaller consulting firms. In larger firms, there are likely HR professionals that assume such responsibilities.

Recruiters working in consulting firms are usually paid a base salary plus a commission or bonus. The bonus may consist of a flat rate for each hire or a variable rate depending upon the position's level of difficulty. Bonuses may also be based upon completed projects or the firm's profits. There may also be team incentives when groups of recruiters reach certain goals. Salaries for recruiters vary widely, again depending upon the recruiter's and firm's performance, market and employment brand, among others.

Summary

In summary, below is a breakdown of the external vs. internal recruiting environments:

<u>External Environments:</u>
- Recruiters work for a third party and provide recruiting services for the benefit of their clients.

- Firms charge fees or bill rates for the candidates they place and/or the services they provide.
- Competition is more fierce as recruiters may compete with several firms to fill one position (while not mentioned previously, recruiters within the same firm may even compete with one another to fill open positions).
- Unlike search firm recruiters, professional staffing firm recruiters should maintain frequent contact with their hires and are responsible for retention.
- Recruiters in this environment are usually paid in the same manner as sales people and therefore, they often receive a commission based upon the individual gross profit they generate.

Internal Environments:

- Recruiters are employees of the company for which they recruit and are not employed by a third party.
- Recruiters don't face external competition when filling positions.
- Internal recruiters may solicit the services of external recruiters, thus becoming the client.
- Unlike most corporate environments, consulting firms deploy their employees to work on external projects.
- Corporate recruiters are primarily compensated with base salaries, but may receive bonuses based upon overall performance; consulting firm recruiters are more likely to receive variable pay (commissions or bonuses for each individual hire) given the nature of their business.

Aside from these environmental differences, recruiters must perform similar responsibilities no matter what the environment. As mentioned earlier, the recruiting competencies for these environments are leveling and recruiters must focus on top performers and quality … in any environment. With that said, the next section will delve into recruiting activities broken down into the recruitment lifecycle.

CHAPTER TWO

Introduction to the Recruitment Lifecycle

You may find varying models of the recruitment lifecycle. Some may be continuous circles, while others appear as charts. Some may combine or break down the different stages or use different labels. For simplicity, the model used here portrays seven stand-alone, successive stages with one support stage revolving around these (see figure 2.1 below).

Figure 2.1 Recruiting Lifecycle

Within each of these stages are a multitude of processes that take place. Before we explore the stages and processes, we must first establish some assumptions, outlined below:

- Workforce planning precedes core recruiting activities (the activities associated with talent acquisition).
- Retention follows core recruiting activities.

  Note: In reality, retention and workforce planning should be performed as ongoing initiatives in parallel to acquiring needed talent.

- There is an open position or a specific workforce "need" that prompts the core recruiting activities to begin.

The darker stages in the center of figure 2.1 are the core recruiting stages while workforce planning and retention are pre-recruiting and post-recruiting stages, respectively. Core recruiting stages refer to the process of acquiring and integrating talent into the workforce. The "pre" and "post" activities are performed, at least to some extent, by recruiters but may be performed in whole or in part by management and human resource professionals as well.

PRE-RECRUITING STAGE

1. **Workforce Planning:** "A systematic, fully integrated organizational process that involves proactively planning ahead to avoid talent surpluses or shortages" (Sullivan, 2002, November, ¶ 2).

CORE RECRUITING STAGES:

2. **Information Gathering:** Gathering the necessary information from the hiring manager in order to perform a targeted search.

3. **Sourcing:** The process of identifying sourcing strategies (planning phase) and implementing that strategy, resulting in a candidate pool.

4. **Selection:** Utilizing a series of tools and/or techniques to determine if the candidate is a fit for the position and company. This phase usually consists of prescreening, presentation to hiring managers and final selection processes to include some or all of the following: formal interviews, skills testing, personality testing, reference checks, drug testing and criminal background checks.

5. **Offer:** Extending the position to the selected candidate, complete with starting salary, expected start date, title and other position details.

6. **Onboarding:** Preparing the future employee to start work (paperwork transactions, orientation, etc.) and initiating his or her integration into the culture.

POST RECRUITING STAGES

7. **Retention:** Simply put, this is an effort to retain employees. Some recruiters are directly involved with this stage, as in professional staffing

firms, and others are indirectly involved. While retention is a "post-recruiting" activity, it directly affects recruiting and has become a viable recruiting strategy (Stevens-Huffman, 2006). This will be discussed as the final stage in the lifecycle.

SUPPORT STAGE

8. Measurement and quality assurance: This is extremely important to the success and performance of the recruitment system and is an ongoing process of measurement and improvement throughout each stage of the lifecycle.

As mentioned, there are a slew of processes that take place within these stages. In fact, Staffing.org has documented 101 recruiting processes! Below is an outline of some of the processes that may occur in each stage. This list is not all inclusive!

Workforce Planning
- Assess and understand corporate strategy
- Assess past workforce trends in promotions, status changes (part-time to full time), exits (those leaving the organization), etc.
- Assess employment growth, business cycles and current vacancies
- Forecast future needs and demands
- Scan the talent pool (both internal and external)
- Develop action plans

Information Gathering
- Review requisitions or job descriptions for current openings
- Meet and form partnership with the hiring manager
- Outline the goals, processes and commitments needed from each party
- Determine the primary and secondary knowledge, skills and abilities (KSA's) the hiring manager is seeking
- Research position and the department (and sometimes company)
- Record position information in recruiting database

Sourcing
- Determine sourcing strategy and search plan

- Prepare and place ads/job postings
- Network
- Solicit referrals
- Conduct special recruiting events (job fairs, campus recruiting, etc.)

Selection

- Prescreen
- Conduct formal interviews
- Conduct skills or personality testing
- Check professional references and work history
- Perform background check and/or drug testing

Offer

- Select candidate for offer
- Make verbal offer
- Negotiate compensation, benefits or other incentives
- Determine start date and other specifics
- Present formal, written offer
- Notify candidates not selected

Onboarding

- Prepare candidate for new hire processes
- Close requisition
- Distribute information to appropriate parties
- Orientation (for some recruiters)
- First day follow up
- New hire processing

Retention

- Place quality employees
- Follow up after employee has settled into their role
- Provide a copy of the new hire satisfaction survey to the hiring manager (allows manager to address any concerns/complaints from the new hire)

<u>Measurement and Quality Assurance</u>
- Record recruiting activities, cost and performance
- Send new hire satisfaction survey (also serves as a retention effort)
- Send quality survey to hiring manager
- Evaluate and measure data/information against goals
- Address performance issues in the recruiting process as needed

(Staffing.org, 2004)

CHAPTER THREE

Stage 1: Workforce Planning

Workforce planning (also referred to as human resource planning) is a systematic and proactive process of forecasting an organization's future talent demand and available talent supply, both internal and external (Sullivan, 2002, November). The following are major components of workforce planning:

- Identify company goals and strategy
- Conduct environmental scan
- Assess potential vacancies through promotion, attrition, new positions, status changes, etc.
- Assess potential surpluses
- Forecast demand
- Assess internal and external talent supply
- Forecast available supply
- Create talent action plans (this may include recruiting, employee development, leadership development, succession planning, redeployment, performance management, retention, outsourcing, etc.)
- Communicate information to appropriate parties to implement and execute action plans
- Measurement and continuous improvement

Workforce planning is most often "owned" by HR with key stakeholders being those responsible for management, recruitment, employee development, retention and succession planning (identifying and developing successors for key positions) among others. It can play a vital role in an organization's performance and success. With that being said, many companies don't perform it at all and of those that do, often don't perform it well. There are many theories for this:

- It's not fully understood by those that are to perform the actual planning
- It's not clearly or consistently defined
- Leadership doesn't understand the contribution it can make to the bottom line and doesn't fully support it
- Being reactive is easier than being proactive
- It takes time and money to do it right
- Workforce planning is more than just analysis and forecasts, it requires action plans and execution
- It can be a complicated and daunting task to implement a "formal" workforce planning program

(Sullivan, 2002, November)

In the last bullet above, "formal" refers to the structured tools, processes and general infrastructure to systematically perform workforce planning. Some of these may include the following:

- Company goal evaluation
- Ratio analysis
- Regression analysis
- Markov analysis
- Manager judgments (subjective top down or bottom up judgments)
- Replacement charts (used in succession planning)
- Internal environmental scans
- External environmental scans (the labor market is most relevant to recruiting)
- Internal skills/competency inventories
- Gap analysis
- Availability analysis (available percentage of women and minorities as compared to how many are actually employed in the organization; often compared in terms of job groups)

- Recruiting objectives
- Recruiting action plans

(Sullivan, 2002, November; "Workforce Planning", 2002)

We'll not delve into the specifics of each of these but more information may be found at the websites for the Society of Workforce Planning Professionals (www.swpp.org) or the Human Resource Planning Society (www.hrps.org). Searches on other human resource and staffing related sites (found in the appendix) will also yield information on this topic. This level of workforce planning is most associated with internal environments, but again, it is often not performed or not performed well for reasons mentioned previously. **Just recently, workforce planning has been recognized as a key strategic advantage and organizations are beginning to take it more seriously.** The bullets below outline why:

- Being prepared is much more efficient and effective than being taken by surprise
- Being reactive costs the company potential talent, which results in lost time and money
- Companies that use workforce planning techniques are often much more competitive than those that don't
- It more accurately prevents surpluses, thus preventing layoffs and negative affects on employee morale and productivity
- It allows you to identify and prevent problems early
- It allows you to be more effective in developing strategy rather than constantly putting out fires

(Sullivan, 2002, November)

While workforce planning programs may be primarily an HR and management initiative, recruiters should also participate in this at some level—if not formally, at least informally (after all, they are considered a part of HR!). If you are in an environment that does perform workforce planning, take the initiative and get involved in the process. **Assessing and understanding business cycles, innovations, new organizational initiatives, new clients and market changes can no doubt benefit recruiters.** For example, technological advances may require new positions or eliminate old positions. This is crucial information for the IT recruiter! If workforce planning isn't performed, again take the initiative. Suggest it to leadership and provide the advantages of implementing it. You may even perform this at the individual level.

Some recruiters, internal or external, may already be performing informal workforce planning and not realize it. They may review positions they've had open with hiring managers in the past. This may uncover peak cycles allowing the recruiter to proactively discuss anticipated needs. They may review and question hiring managers about upcoming key initiatives and projects requiring additional employees. They may assess if their company (or clients for external recruiters) is experiencing an increase in business or a change in products/services that will require additional talent. They may examine their talent supply and determine KSA's that align with hiring managers' previous needs then proactively market them.

"Workforce planning forces everyone to begin looking toward the future" and prepare (Sullivan, 2002, November, last paragraph). It allows you to take advantage of opportunities and minimize problems. **To be a high performance recruiter, you must be proactive, plan and take action!**

CHAPTER FOUR

Stage 2: Information Gathering

Information gathering begins the core recruiting activities. Once the recruiter is alerted that a position is open (recall that this assumption was made for purposes of simplicity) the recruiter should carefully review the requisition, if one is available, and **gather the information needed to perform a targeted search.** The key word here is "targeted." Recruiters may perform a search with some high level information provided in a job description but this may prove to be ineffective, inefficient and may solidify the recruiter as just an order taker. **High performance recruiters know that to be most effective, they must develop a partnership with the hiring manager and determine what is actually needed versus the "nice to haves".** For example:

- List the top five primary activities for this position and an approximate percentage of time allotted to each.
- What are the most important hard skills a candidate must already possess for this position? Least important? Which ones may be learned or developed on the job?
- If I find A & B, but not C (or other combination), would you still like to see the candidate?
- Is the education requirement a deal breaker or could experience substitute?
- What soft skills (for example, attention to detail) are imperative for a candidate to already possess? Which ones are least important or may be developed?
- Will there be training for certain skills a candidate may lack?

- What are the overall goals of this position? How will the person in this position contribute to the company's goals or bottom line?
- Why is this position open, e.g., is it a newly created position? Did someone leave? If someone vacated the position, why?
- Who does this position report to (both directly and indirectly)? Will this person have direct reports? Indirect reports?
- With what other positions (titles) would this person be closely working?
- What is your time frame for filling this position?
- Other than X, Y or Z is there any other specific organizations, networking circles, direct or indirect competitors (for search firm recruiters) that may prove to be useful in sourcing qualified candidates? *This question is primarily for recruiters that are new to a specific type of position, skill set or even client.* *

* It is important to note that this question is utilized to develop a thorough sourcing strategy and is not intended to ask the hiring manager all the sources that should be utilized. This is the recruiter's job to determine!

Recruiters should also know the business dynamics, processes and general information of the department and company. Depending upon the environment or situation, this information may already be known. For example, corporate recruiters should already know most information about their company and the departments for which they recruit. However, there may be circumstances when they are unfamiliar with department or project details, especially if the recruiter is new to a specific group. Search firm recruiters should ask such questions of each new hiring manager. However, if the recruiter has worked with the hiring manager in the past, this information should already be in the recruiting database or client management system. Professional staffing firm recruiters should also obtain this information since their employee will be working at the client's worksite and under the client's supervision. However, because they are the employer, they should also provide similar information about their own firm. Below is a sample of questions to ask in order to uncover key company and departmental information:

- What is your specific title and what is your role (or department's role) in the organization?
- What products/services does your company offer?

- What is your annual revenue?
- In how many markets are you established?
- What is the company's culture?
- What is the department's culture?
- What are some company awards, honors, innovations, changes, etc. that would make employees excited to work for you?
- What is the structure of your organization and more specifically, your department?
- How many people are in the department? Company?
- What is your selection process? With whom will candidates be interviewing? Do you require multiple interviews? Panel interviews? Skills testing? Background checks? Drug Test?

During this stage, salary ranges and bill rates must also be confirmed in order to prevent any wasted time during the search, selection and offer stages. For example, the hiring manager provides a salary range of $80–$100,000. She may really mean, "I only have a budget for $80,000–$85,000 and this is the range I prefer." You should "smoke" these out in the beginning to save time going forward. A good follow up question is, **"Just to confirm, if I find a qualified candidate that is seeking a minimum of $100,000, this is an acceptable salary."** Gauge her confirmation of this statement and determine if the highest range is indeed acceptable. You may even want to probe further to determine if she is willing to see candidates just outside this range. For example, **"If I find a superstar with A, B, and C with X experience in the specific industry, but his salary requirement is firm at 110k, would you still wish to see his resume?"** The same holds true for staffing firm recruiters working with bill rates. Always confirm the high end of the range.

Recruiters must also gather and understand the benefits, stock options, bonuses or other incentives that may lure candidates, especially if they want to attract top talent. These along with base salary make up the entire package and will not only attract top candidates, but may be helpful if pay must be negotiated. For example, if a company covers 100% of the health premiums, candidates should know this! Health plans and healthcare contributions may be a primary motivator for some candidates. They may even be willing to negotiate salary given the benefits or other inducements offered. Keep in mind that these may not sway the candidate at all (or very little) and will depend upon each individual circumstance. However, **high performance recruiters gather this information, understand the monetary value and effectively communicate it to their candidates. They use this as leverage when pay must be negotiated.**

The information obtained during this stage is not only viable for the recruiter to target appropriate candidates, but candidates will likely ask similar questions of the recruiter. A prepared recruiter with this information is much more respected than the recruiter that says, "Let's just schedule the interview and you can ask those questions of the hiring manager." You will get bitten on this! The candidate may interview and feel as though he wasted his time because the appropriate information wasn't provided up front. This gives the recruiter and the company a bad reputation for being unprepared and lazy. You not only risk this with the candidate, but with the people he talks to, including other professionals in his network. However, there will be times when the candidate asks a question and the answer isn't readily available. **Be honest! Make every effort to find out and get back to him. Make a list of questions in which you need to follow up and ensure you contact the candidate in a timely manner.**

While managers are busy, it is important that they understand that recruiters represent their position and their company. Therefore, recruiters should make every effort to meet with their hiring managers. **This provides insight into the work environment, team, operations and culture. It will also allow the recruiter to gain an understanding of the hiring manager's personality and leadership style. Finally, meeting the hiring manager face-to-face builds better rapport.**

Lastly and preferably during the initial meeting, **it's important that the recruiter discusses the recruitment process, timeframes and responsibilities of each party** (see figure 4.1). The hiring manager must understand what's expected of her, as well as what she can expect from the recruiter. This is especially true if you're recruiting for a hiring manager for the first time. Expectations should surround response times and feedback, among others. If response times are long, good candidates may be lost and the position delayed. Therefore, timely response times must be established to curtail such incidents. **The target response times for both parties should be within 24 or 48 hours** but should not be more than 72 hours. Feedback from the hiring manager is also extremely important. This information assists the recruiter in sourcing and selecting the right candidates. Therefore, recruiters must establish the need for detailed feedback so the search may be a success.

In addition, key measures of success should be discussed and agreed upon between both parties in order to measure and ensure the quality of service. It's also helpful to establish key milestones, along with their projected time frames. **The most important milestone that should be established, however, is the projected time to start.** This is referred to as the "contracted time to start" by Staffing.org in the *Staffing Metrics Toolkit*. Contracted time to start is a reasonable and concrete date that is established and agreed upon by both recruiter and hiring manager. It is then used to measure an aspect of the recruiter's performance by comparing the "actual time to start vs. contracted time to start" (Staffing.org, 2006, p. 17). This is discussed in more detail in Chapter Ten.

The information gathering stage is extremely important as it provides a well-rounded knowledge base that should be used to target and attract the best candidates for the position. Furthermore, it sets the stage for other logistics and expectations, allowing for accountability, quality, trust and teamwork. **High performance recruiters utilize this opportunity to develop partnerships with hiring managers and make the process more effective and efficient for all involved, including candidates.**

Figure 4.1

Sample Recruitment Agreement

COMPANY LOGO

GENERAL INFORMATION		
Hiring Manager Name/Title:	**Position Title:**	**Division:**
John Smith, VP of IT	IT Director	Software Development
Recruiter Name:	**Date Received:**	**Priority (high/med./low):**
Recruiter X	11/1/2007	High
RECRUITER AGREEMENT		

Recruiter Deliverables:

- Set up meeting within 2 days of receiving the requisition to:
    - Outline the recruitment process
    - Discuss search plan
    - Discuss a targeted time to start date: 3/1/2008
    - Identify the parties involved in the interview process
    - Determine methods of communication and follow up
- Prescreen and forward qualified candidates to the Hiring Manager
- Schedule interviews for candidates
- With the Hiring Manager, evaluate candidates that have been interviewed
- Extend offer and communicate status to the Hiring Manager
- Initiate onboarding process

Key Milestones:	Targeted Completion Dates:
• Qualified resumes prescreened and forwarded	• As received, but qualified candidates received no later than 11/30/2007
• First interviews scheduled	• 12/1–12/20/2007
• Second interviews scheduled	• 1/3–1/24/2008
• Final selection criteria completed	• 1/24–2/14/2008
• Offer made	• 2/15/2008
• Start Date (contracted time to start)	• 3/1/2008

Key Measurements:

- Actual time to start vs. the contracted time to start
- Total number (minimum of three) and types of sourcing tactics used
- Quality of candidates referred (do they meet the requirements?)
- Recruiter response time and follow up (within 24 hours)
- Quality of candidate hired (as determined by selection criteria)

HIRING MANAGER AGREEMENT

Hiring Manager Deliverables:

- Respond to the recruiter within 48 hours of receiving a resume to provide feedback
- Respond to the recruiter within 48 hours of an interview to provide feedback
- Be reasonably available to interview each candidate in a timely manner
- With the recruiter, evaluate candidates that have been interviewed
- Provide prompt offer/onboarding information

CHAPTER FIVE

Stage 3: Sourcing

The sourcing stage is the process of determining the appropriate locations (sources) to find suitable candidates, then from these, developing an active talent pool. This stage consists of two phases, which are detailed below:

a. Planning

Selectively determining the best and most cost-effective sourcing tactics/resources based upon position requirements & information gathering.

b. Search

Applying and following through with the sourcing plan, resulting in an active talent pool. The list below consists of some of the more popular recruiting sources:

- **Job Postings**

    Pro: Candidates come to you so you know they are interested in the position.

    Con: Potentially produces an overload of unqualified candidates.

  - Monster.com
  - Careerbuilder.com
  - Hot Jobs.com
  - Company Careers Site
  - Organization web sites (i.e., PMI, SHRM, etc.)
  - Other niche sites that you may wish to purchase

- **Database Mining**

  Pro: You target the candidates you feel are qualified.

  Con: You may find that some are not interested in your position. *NOTE: Search agents should always be set up as databases are mined.*

  - Monster.com
  - Dice.com (an IT job board and candidate database)
  - Careerbuilder.com
  - Hotjobs.com
  - 6figurejobs.com (a job board and candidate database focusing on six figure salaries)
  - Company database
  - Other niche databases

- **Referrals**

  Pro: Candidates are typically high quality.

  Con: You may find that some are not interested in your position or are sometimes unqualified. Referrals may be solicited from:

  - Current employees
  - Individuals in company database
  - Individuals in other candidate databases
  - Professional organizations
  - Other organizations such as church, alumni associations, user groups, social groups, etc.

- **Networking**

  Pro: Can produce quality candidates.

  Con: Requires more long-term investment of your time.

  - Professional organizations
  - Personal network of professional contacts
  - Other organizations such as church, alumni associations, user groups, social groups, etc.

- Internet networks, such as Linked In (www.linkedin.com) and Ryze (www.ryze.com)

- **Cold Calling**

  Pro: Can produce quality candidates that other firms aren't actively recruiting.

  Con: Takes a lot of time and calls to find someone with the right qualifications and interested in making a move.

  NOTE: It is important to always ask for referrals when cold calling!

  - Targeting local or national companies in the industry
  - Performing internet searches (spiders, web-crawlers, flipping or x-raying)
  - Purchasing organization lists
  - Purchasing company organization charts
  - Utilizing research vendors to compile targeted lists
  - Calling references provided by previous candidates or those listed on resumes from candidate databases

- **Job Fairs**

  Pro: Promotes name/brand recognition.

  Con: May produce a lot of unqualified, unmanageable paper resumes. *NOTE: Resumes may be more easily managed if the job fair CD or online database (with all resumes) is purchased.*

  - Niche professional job fairs (IT, engineering, healthcare, etc.)
  - College job fairs
  - Minority related job fairs
  - General city sponsored or chamber of commerce job fairs
  - Employer sponsored job fairs, also known as "open houses"

- **Campus/College Recruiting** *HIGH SCHOOL*

  Pro: Promotes name/brand recognition; potential to solicit sharp and eager candidates.

  Con: Candidates may not have the qualifications for many upper level or other highly skilled positions.

  - Local universities and colleges
  - National universities or colleges
  - National universities or colleges with top degree programs in a specific profession

- **Print Advertising**

  Pro: Promotes name/brand recognition & solicits good candidates for many professions.

  Con: May receive unqualified resumes; some candidates don't always look in the paper where the position is located (newspapers don't have a broad net to reach candidates in other cities). Trade magazines and other publications may be very expensive.

  - Local newspapers - *LEO / COFFEE NEWS*
  - Trade magazines
  - Professional organization publications

- **Other Sources**
  - Researching company layoffs and soliciting downsized employees
  - Flyers
  - Walk-ins or word-of-mouth
  - Radio or TV advertising
  - For internal recruiters:
    - Search firms or professional staffing firms
    - Hiring independent contractors/consultants already on staff

Planning

The template in figure 5.1 will assist in navigating this step of the Search Stage. It is filled out based upon a "phantom" opening, but will serve as an example of what to include as you assess your position. If you're new to recruiting, a specific industry or position, it is recommended that you use this template or one similar in order to plan and evaluate the search tactics for a given position. Most of this may be filled out from the information obtained during the information gathering stage and if necessary, with further internet or general research. If you are a search or professional staffing firm recruiter, something you should take into account is the sourcing tactics the client may have already used. For example, if the client has already used sources and have had no success, you may want to refrain from using these sources yourself.

The recruiter should obtain as much of this information on his or her own or through the information gathering stage. Recruiters should not have to schedule follow up calls or meetings to obtain this information, although it may be appropriate to clarify terms or concepts that are vague or unfamiliar. This template is a tool that should be used internally by the recruiter to assist in the search process. Therefore, it should never be filled out by the hiring manager!

This template is only a guide and is very helpful to those that are new to recruiting or new to a specific position or industry. Recruiters will find that with experience, they rely less on the template as these questions will become second nature.

Figure 5.1: Search Template Example

Search Template	
POSITION: Senior Developer	CLIENT: XYZ insurance

Position Research	
"Must Have" Key Words:	C#, SQL
Synonyms to Key Words:	Sequel, visualstudio.net
Preferred Key Words:	Vb.net, ado.net
Industry Terms:	Sarbanes Oxley, HIPAA, billing, enrollment, claims
Similar Titles:	Developer, programmer, software engineer

Sourcing Plan	
Job boards and databases:	Monster, Dice, internal database & company website for posting
Print:	Local IT group newsletter
Organizations:	Local & national C# users' groups
Referral contacts:	This should be specific names that are in your network and/or you've contacted previously about positions—look at the history of old job orders, etc. to develop a list of candidates and people to contact to get referrals.
Colleges:	N/A (this isn't applicable to colleges since a senior level candidate is being sought)
Websites:	This could be any resume url's you've come across, free posting sites, niche sites, developer's blogs, networking sites, etc.
Companies/Competitors:	This area may be used to identify companies that may be going through a lay-off, going out of business, etc. that may have employees actively seeking positions. It is also appropriate for search firm recruiters (or other recruiters) using cold calling tactics.
Search radius:	This depends upon the ability and desire to relocate someone. It may depend upon the budget and/or the ability to find someone in the local market.
Other:	This is for other sourcing opportunities not mentioned above. For example, an IT job fair.
Search Outcome/Comments:	This field is used for "lessons learned" after the search is completed. Did you fill the position? If so, where did you find the candidate(s)? Where did you find the most candidates? Where did you find the best candidates? Did you use a source that was unsuccessful? Did a competitor fill the position? Why? What did they do that you didn't?

Search

After the planning phase, it's time to begin the search. There are many search tactics and sourcing options as previously outlined. In this section, the most common sources will be reviewed.

Job Board Posting

Being proactive is emphasized throughout this book and is one of the key ingredients of high performance recruiting. However, placing ads isn't considered proactive and you may wonder why this is being discussed. It's important to leverage proactive and "reactive" sourcing tactics and utilize both when appropriate. Posting positions (or ads) may yield good results for certain positions. It also communicates employment brand and advertises the company, serving more than just one purpose. Not to mention, most companies have a careers page on their company website in which recruiters must (or should) post all open positions.

The first step in implementing your sourcing strategy may likely be posting the position in your recruiting database, which in turn, posts to your company's careers page (with the right technology). Job ads are an art and a science. While companies still place paper ads, there are many benefits to posting online: 1) you are not limited in space as you are with paper ads, 2) online postings are generally cheaper, 3) links to online applications, your company's website, benefits information, etc. are more easily accessible and 4) employment brand is more easily marketed. When posting an online (or a paper) ad, use vocabulary and imagery to grab and hold the reader's attention. For example:

- Provide positive information about your company, what it does, products, services, initiatives or what sets the company apart from others, allowing the reader to understand some of the reasons why they may want to work there
- Explain how the position impacts the company's bottom line to show its value to the organization
- Use key word terms
- Utilize strong action verbs or adjectives when describing responsibilities

- Don't be so detailed that it is boring, but provide enough information to gain the reader's interest
- Utilize bullets or bold so responsibilities and/or qualifications may be easily scanned
- Provide pay ranges and/or other attractive incentives and benefits

(Weddle, 2003, ¶ 9)

While many companies don't provide pay ranges, there is some evidence to suggest that people are more likely to respond to an ad when this is included (Weddle, 2003, ¶ 10). You're also more likely to target those in the right pay range from the start, thus saving time during the prescreen. However, many companies fear that other employees will see this information and become disgruntled. It may also set an expectation for candidates. For example, if a range of $50,000–$70,000 per year is provided, most will focus on and expect closer to $70,000. An option for posting specific pay ranges may be to state, "competitive pay" and be more detailed with benefits and other incentives.

Database Mining

Mining internet databases or search engines require knowledge of Boolean operators. **Boolean operators allow you to pinpoint information and weed out irrelevant data.** The Recruiters Network (www.recruitersnetwork.com) has provided a summary of Boolean key operators and a quick search guide for various search engines. Figures 5.2 and 5.3 provide this information (the specific link may be obtained from the "References" section of this book).

Figure 5.2: Recruiters Network Resource for Boolean Operators

AND—The AND operator delivers results with the terms you requested. For example, searching resume and oracle will return pages with both terms-resume and oracle.

OR—The OR operator delivers results with either of the terms you requested. For example, MCSE OR M.C.S.E.

NOT—The NOT operator will not deliver certain words in your search results. For example, Java NOT coffee will deliver closer results for JAVA Programmers and not Java Coffee.

NEAR—The NEAR operator locates words that are located in close proximity to other words. For example, Java NEAR Programmer. Not every search engine supports this operator.

() Parentheses—The () operator allows you to group terms and build longer search strings. For example, NOT (submit AND employer) will avoid pages with both names.

*—The * operator is a wild card. Adding a wild card will find words contain the wild card. For example program* will help so you do not have to run separate searches for words similar like: programmer, programming, program

Example of Complex Search String: resume AND (java or JavaScript) AND program* AND (New York or NY or 212) AND NOT (coffee or submit)

> * In some case we recommend to go to the advanced search option within the search engine.

> *This information was reprinted with permission.*

Figure 5.3 Recruiters Network Search Engine Quick Guide

.	AltaVista	HotBot	Go *	Northern Light	Snap
AND	resume AND oracle +resume +oracle	resume AND oracle	+resume +oracle	resume AND oracle +resume +oracle	resume AND oracle
OR	resume OR oracle	resume OR oracle	Default is OR automatically	resume OR oracle	resume OR oracle
NEAR	oracle NEAR programmming (finds words within 10 words of each other)	Not Supported	Not Supported	Not Supported	Not Supported
" "	"sales manager"	Select "Exact Phrase"	"Document must contain exact phrase"	"sales manager"	Select "Exact Phrase"
( )	resume AND (sales OR "sales manager")	resume AND (sales OR "sales manager")	Not Supported	resume AND (sales OR "sales manager")	resume AND (sales OR "sales manager")
* (Wild Card)	develop* (finds develop or developer or any other word starting with develop)	Not Supported	Not Supported	* replaces multiple characters, % replaces one character	Not Supported
Field Searches	.	.	.	.	.
X-Ray	host:website.com	domain:website.com	"url must contain" website.com	"words in url" website.com	domain:website.com
Flip Search	link:website.com	"links to this url" http://www.website.com	"hyperlink must contain the words" website.com	link:anysite.com	"links to this url" http://www.website.com
Page Title Search	title: resume	"words in the page title" resume	"title must contain" resume	"words in the title" resume	"words in the page title" resume
URL Search	url:resume	Not Supported	"url must contain the words" resume	"words in url" resume	Not Supported

Definitions:
- X-Raying—searches for pages that are all on the same host.
- Flipping—searches for pages that link to a specific page.
- Page Title—searches for pages that have specific words in page title.
- URL Search—searches for pages that have specific words in the URL or web address.

* "InfoSeek" from the original source is now "Go" found at www.go.com.

This information was reprinted with permission.

Notice the "field searches" category near the bottom of the guide in figure 5.3 (5th category from the bottom). These are search strings used to search pages "behind" or linked to main web pages. These are often used to find passive candidates by means of resume links, employee profiles, bibliographies or other information that may be written about organizations' employees or other skilled individuals.

Networking and Referrals

When it comes to networking and referrals, **remember that *everyone* may know of someone. Make it a habit to ask for referrals even when you don't have a specific position in mind.** The candidates in your recruiting database make good contacts for referrals. **Offer referral bonuses! This is the best way to motivate people!**

It is also extremely beneficial to join organizations specializing in the profession(s) in which you recruit. For example, if you recruit actuaries or underwriters, you should join such professional organizations and attend the meetings or conferences. This will not only allow you to network with these professionals, but you'll broaden your knowledge of the field and gain credibility with your candidates. It is difficult to recruit professionals without knowing what they do, the challenges they face, trends, hot buttons, etc. and organizations will provide all this information along with a solid network of potential candidates and/or a source for referrals.

Recruiters also benefit from online social networks. These allow recruiters to stay connected with a group of people electronically. The people in your network may also have a network with whom you may connect. Sending a request for referrals for your position(s) through this type of network will reach many individuals that may actually elicit some great candidates.

Another good source for referrals is the references that previous or current candidates have provided. When contacting a reference, conclude by asking if she may know of anyone for an ongoing need or if she knows anyone for a specific opening. Solicit referrals in line with the reference's profession. For example, if the reference is a nurse and you're a healthcare recruiter, ask her if she knows of any nurses, physicians, physical therapists, etc. that may be interested in positions you have available. You may actually find that she's interested, which is a great opportunity to ask for her resume and discuss the position in more detail. She may also provide a referral or even two. The worst that can happen in this situation is that she blows you off. This shouldn't be taken personally. Take it at face value and simply thank her for providing the reference information.

One final note on this topic—be proactive with your network of people. Check in with them from time to time even when you don't need a referral. Be an active member of professional organizations, user groups and social or personal networks rather than just having the goal of soliciting candidates. In other words, **take interest in the professions for which you recruit and maintain contact with your network(s)!**

Campus Recruiting

When your position calls for an entry level candidate, student or recent graduate, campus recruiting is a valuable resource. When considering the campuses in which to recruit, it is best to target your efforts and focus on those that have programs in your specialty area. For example, if you are a recruiter that specializes in engineering, you'll want to target the local or regional colleges or universities that have such programs. Research colleges or universities nationwide and determine those that have top 20 programs. There are also minority colleges and universities that you should target as these may provide quality candidates and promote a diverse workforce.

There are job boards and networks that allow you to specifically post positions with college/university career centers. These may be an efficient means to communicate openings for several colleges' students or alumni. Otherwise, you should keep in close contact with individual career centers and attend campus recruiting events in order to solicit these potential candidates.

Job Fairs

Likewise, when selecting the job fairs you wish to attend, you should target those in your specialty area (the professions for which you recruit). If you recruit medical professionals, target the healthcare job fairs and pay close attention to the other companies that will be in attendance. For example, if a top medical facility (e.g., Johns Hopkins Hospital) is going to be in attendance, they will likely draw an excellent pool of medical professionals. Therefore, if you're a healthcare recruiter, you may want to consider a booth at that job fair!

If you are in a small to medium city general job fairs may produce a quality pool of professionals, and in addition, will increase brand recognition in your local area. When considering a general job fair, the same rule applies for specialty job fairs. Pay close attention to the other companies that will be in attendance. If a large local company with an excellent brand name in your community is attending, you may want to attend that job fair as well, especially if you don't have a specialty area and recruit for all professions. Minority job fairs are also extremely valuable in finding quality candidates and promoting a diverse workforce. These should also be researched and considered when selecting the job fair(s) you wish to attend.

Job fairs may not be a viable option for many positions and they do require considerable time and money. They don't necessarily produce the types of candidates recruiters are seeking. They may also produce candidates that can be obtained from more cost-effective sources. For these reasons, many organizations are going the way of the Internet to source candidates. However, an option that many job fair organizations offer is a resume CD or database. When attendees register, their resumes are stored on CD or in an online database and sold to interested organizations. This is a convenient and cost-effective option if you are unsure of the job fair or if you want to test it out to determine the caliber of applicants it draws.

The greatest benefit of job fairs is brand recognition and marketing. You're not only marketed in local newspapers and publications by the job fair organization, but you're marketing and creating brand recognition to all those in attendance. Another benefit is that you actually get to meet the people that are interested in your organization. If you do decide that a job fair will be beneficial to your search, take advantage of the interview rooms that most job fairs provide and expedite the prescreening or interview process!

Cold Calling

Last but not least is cold calling. Cold calling is an art that takes lots of practice to master. A recruiter must be comfortable speaking with a prospect that may be on the defense and have a way of keeping him or her engaged. Not to mention, the recruiter must first master the art of getting past the gatekeeper! This tactic is used mostly by search firm recruiters but may be performed by other recruiters as well.

This method takes time, skill and may take many, many tries to find an interested and qualified candidate for the immediate position. In addition, some cold calling tactics are considered unethical because some recruiters will pretend to be in a situation that they're not in order to reach the appropriate person. For example, receptionists or administrative assistants may be trained to deter these "headhunters" (search firm recruiters) from soliciting the company's employees. Recruiters may make up stories that they need to reach accounts payable. The call is forwarded and once they reach the accounts payable representative, they say they've been incorrectly transferred and need to be connected to the controller—Mr. Jones. Accounts payable representatives, unaware of the true intent, will likely correct the name and transfer them!

There are more ethical means of cold calling than the example provided above. **You may get names of professionals from company websites, professional lists, general articles and referrals. You may also find that candidates voluntarily include references on their applications, resume submittals or on their online resumes. These references may be the candidate you're looking for! You may call him or her directly and be up front about why you're calling.** For example:

> *My name is _____ and I'm with _____. I was referred to you by (the source in which the name was obtained). My client has an excellent*

opportunity for a _____ paying as much as $x. Do you know of any-
one that may be qualified and interested in the position?

In this scenario, you may get a "no, I'm not interested" then a dial tone. If you're able to keep her on the line for a few seconds, ask if she may have any referrals. Let her know that you'll pay a referral bonus if she refers someone that you place. Referral bonuses are very useful motivators when attempting to solicit names, not to mention they're cost-effective. You may possibly intrigue the prospect enough that she asks more questions. She may eventually become interested herself, which is the ultimate goal. However, in these instances, you don't always know if she meets all the qualifications. Ask for a resume and ask more background questions to determine if she's really a viable candidate.

Cold calling takes a lot of time and hard work, but with practice and determination, you are likely to get high quality candidates for your position. You also develop a network of contacts in which to call in the future, so **don't discard any names or numbers you've obtained**!

CHAPTER SIX

Stage 4: Selection

Selection is the process of determining the best candidate for the position. The selection process includes resume/application reviews, prescreening (a form of interviewing), interviews, skills testing, personality testing, drug tests, criminal background checks, reference and work history checks and any other instruments, checks, tests, etc. that may be used to select the best candidate(s) for a given position. After applications and/or resumes have been reviewed, recruiters contact those that match the position criteria. This selection step is called the prescreen.

PRESCREENING

Prescreening is the initial contact made with an applicant to determine if he or she meets the qualifications for the position. For example, questions asked of candidates may include:

- What is your compensation requirement?
- Are you willing to travel?
- Do you possess X experience? How many years? What are some of the duties you've performed?
- How proficient are you with X? Provide examples of accomplishments you've achieved in this area.
- Do you have supervisory experience? Where? How many years experience do you have? How many direct reports did (or do) you have?

Other questions related to specific skills, experience and education should also be asked. After conducting the prescreen, the recruiter must determine if the candidate is a fit and provide the relevant information (prescreen summary and resume) to the hiring manager.

Many companies are automating the prescreen process. This is because recruiters are often inundated with applicants and such automation allows the recruiter to be more efficient. Some prescreen technologies include pre-screen questionnaires that are required when applicants apply to an online posting. Some simply transmit the information with the resumes while others rank applicants according to their answers. Other companies may use key word filters. This technology scans resumes and filters out candidates that don't have designated key words on their resume. Automation in the application and prescreening stage is recommended, where appropriate, to effectively manage your time. **These tools will help you weed out the enormous amount of applicants that may apply and help you focus on the ones that do meet the initial criteria.**

Even when automation is used for prescreening, it is still necessary for recruiters to conduct their own prescreen. Why? The reasons are similar to the purpose of discussing an opening with a hiring manager during the information gathering stage.

- To confirm the information you've received
- To develop a relationship
- To probe deeper into answers that may not be clear
- To ask follow up questions, if needed
- To address red flags
- To let candidates know your interest level
- To let the candidate know next steps, if any

Red flags may be gaps in employment, employment in a field unrelated to career, possible demotions or terminations, etc. For certain positions, you will also need to determine the candidate's communication skills. For example, if you're recruiting for a professional trainer and the candidate can barely articulate his work history, then it may be difficult for him to stand in front of a group of people and articulate learning concepts. You should also be careful about blindly presenting a candidate based upon information written on paper (or online). Some candidates may be very good at research then composing the information in writing. However, he may not be able to actively and intelligently discuss some key aspects of the position. Therefore, always speak with candidates and perform your due diligence before presenting to the hiring manager.

Since prescreening is a form of interviewing (and is often a precursor to in-depth, formal interviewing) the following guidelines are essential for recruiters to understand and follow during the prescreening and/or interviewing phases.

- *Prepare!* Understand the key terms and responsibilities of the position and be sure to ask specific questions related to the position. Research the position title or responsibilities prior to talking to your candidate. Be prepared to give a background of your company and what differentiates you from other companies.

    Note: If you are an external recruiter, do not give away your client's name at this point! You don't want applicants applying directly to the Client and going around you!

- *Always give a thorough introduction*—when calling a candidate, explain who you are, who your company is (if you're an external recruiter, this refers to your firm—not your client) and why you're contacting her. For example, if sourced from an internet job board, let her know this. Continue by asking if she has time to talk about the available position. If so, explain the position details and what attracted you to her resume. For example, she has a wealth of cost accounting experience in the manufacturing industry. If this isn't a good time for her, schedule a time that works for both of you, preferably as soon as possible. **Good candidates aren't on the market for very long!**

- *Listen*—don't interrupt or hurry the candidate, but at the same time, keep him or her focused on the questions. **Apply the 80/20 rule** here—the candidate does 80% of the talking and you do 20%.

- *Probe*—if the candidate isn't directly answering the question, probe deeper. Rephrase a statement and ask him to explain in more detail. **Ask** him to explain direct responsibilities and contributions on a project if he uses the term "we" a lot. Keep your ears open for red flags or caveats that may indicate that he's not a fit for the position. Extract accomplishments or bottom line results that may indicate his ability to perform in the role you have available. Ensure this information is presented to the hiring manager.

- *Keep it legal!*—Don't ask inappropriate questions related to ethnicity, gender, marital status, family status, religion, hobbies, or anything personal that is unrelated to the position. There are some positions for the government or other institutions in which some of these items may be a bona fide job requirement (e.g., gender or US citizenship). You will know these up front from the specifications of the job description or work statement. You may also need to get some of this information for EEO purposes, but always make it clear that EEO information is optional and is not used to select candidates.

Below are items **you should not ask**. This list is not all inclusive!

- What is your maiden name?
- Where were you born?
- Where were your parents born?
- What religion are you?
- What church do you attend?
- What social organizations are you a member of?
- What is the color of your skin?
- What is your height?
- What is your weight?
- What is your age?
- Are you married?
- Do you have children?
- What gender are you?
- Are you a US citizen?
- What country are you from?
- What is your medical history?
- Have you ever been arrested?

Keep in mind that there are legal forms of some of these questions, given the information is required for the position. For example, you may ask about convictions as opposed to arrests. Rather than asking a specific age, you may ask if the candidate is over the age of eighteen ("Illegal Interview Questions," 2001). A point of concern for many people often relates to citizenship. You may not ask if a person is a U.S. citizen and you should never make assumptions based upon a person's name or work history. The question to use in this situation is, "Are you authorized to work in the U.S.?" ("Illegal Interview Questions," 2001, ¶ 2). Sponsorship may also be an option, so don't automatically rule out candidates holding a work visa, especially if the position is going to be very difficult to fill.

- *Next Steps*: Always let your candidate know what will happen next. **You may have found that she's not a fit for the position and it's ok to tell her this in a tactful way.** For example, you may have found that her goals don't coincide with the organization's goals. If you have an opening for a "heads down" programmer and she wants to be involved in software design, testing and customer interaction, then she's not a fit for that position. Kindly explain it to her and discuss any other positions that might be a better fit. Think of potential areas that may utilize her skills or of hiring managers that have needed similar skills in the past. If there are possibilities, let her know that you'd like to stay in touch. Flag her resume in your database as a reminder to stay in contact. Ask her to periodically follow up with you or check your website. If she is a good fit for the current opening, inform her that you'll be presenting her information to the hiring manager and you'll be in contact as soon as you receive feedback. Provide your contact information in case she wishes to follow up with you.

- *Manage your time effectively!* You may discover that a candidate is not a fit for a position during the interview, as mentioned in the example above. The candidate may be a fit for other positions or may be very marketable, so in these cases, continue through with the entire interview. However, **you may wish to cut your questions short in cases where the candidate is just failing miserably.** Perhaps he's not as technically inclined as his resume portrays or there is poor communication when the position calls for an excellent communicator. **Whatever the reason, you may need to apply the short version interview.**

Also, you won't be able to assist all candidates you interview and you should be up front with these individuals. This occurs most often for those applicants who aren't in the field in which you're recruiting and/or whose skills aren't marketable to your hiring managers. You should store his resume in the database as a courtesy and because you never know what may come up in the future. He may even be able to provide referrals as recruiters often use mass emails to solicit referrals from people in their database. As mentioned earlier, anyone may know of someone. **However, you should let him know why you're unable to assist him. Direct him to other resources that might be more appropriate for his background.** This should be sufficient information and feedback he appreciates.

While prescreens are most often conducted over the phone, this guideline may also be used when conducting a prescreen or interview face-to-face. If you are conducting the prescreen face-to-face, ensure the candidate is comfortable and be as pleasant as possible. Offer a beverage and warm up with small talk to break the ice.

BEGINNING THE PHONE INTERVIEW:
- Introduce yourself
- Explain why you're contacting the candidate, for example, "You submitted your resume for our "x" opening.…"
- Outline the Agenda:
  - "First I'd like to briefly tell you about us and the opportunity …"
  - "Then, I'd like you to provide some information about your background, skills, etc."
  - "We'll wrap up the interview with any questions you may have."

ABOUT US:
- Provide the name of your company (if you're an external recruiter, this is the company you work for, not the name of your client!), where you're located, and the services or products you provide; include any additional information you feel necessary, e.g., "We're a fortune 100 company …"

- Provide a brief overview of the position.

   NOTE: If the candidate applied for the position, this should be a refresher of the job posting or ad and should be brief. If you sourced the candidate on your own you will need to spend more time on this topic.

ABOUT YOU:

- Start with any position requirements in which the candidate would need to comply (e.g., relocation, being on-call, non-standard hours, etc.)
- Discuss the candidate's current position (or in some cases, their most relevant position)
   - "Summarize what you did."
   - "What were your day to day responsibilities?"
   - Probe for specifics with re: to hard skills, soft skills and area(s) of expertise.
   - What were your greatest accomplishments in this specific role? As a professional in this field?

- What was your reason for leaving or why do you want to leave?
- Discuss any gaps in employment.
- Why are you interested in working for us?
- What would you be able to contribute in this position?
- Discuss what he or she desires in a position:
   - "Desired compensation?"
   - "What do you like doing most? Least?"

   NOTE: If you're an external recruiter, you'll want to probe the following to have a general profile of your candidate to match to future openings:

   - Desired location or commute time.
   - Are you willing to relocate?
   - What percentage of time are you willing to travel?
   - What type of company or industry do you prefer?

- Are there any companies you don't want to work for?
- "We would like to be proactive and collect your references. Please provide at least 2 supervisory references that we may contact." **This is also a source for business leads!**
- If we have positions that match your preferences, may we submit your resume on your behalf? *Be sure to remind the candidate that clients do not receive any contact information.*

CLOSING:
- Is there anything else you'd like to add or any questions you have of me?
- Next Steps

Once you have prescreened a candidate and feel he or she is a fit for the position, you must then present the information to the hiring manager (in some cases, an account manager). To do so, you should provide a summary of the information you obtained and be thorough, relevant and to-the-point. Hiring managers are very busy and don't want to read a history book, so to speak. **A good rule of thumb is one to three paragraphs. Use bullet points, key words or bold to make skills or accomplishments stand out.**

You should start with the basics, which may include some or all of the following:

- Type of position sought
- Desired compensation (or bill rate for professional staffing firms)
- Geographical location
- Willingness to relocate (if applicable)
- Why the candidate is interested in the position
- Availability

You should then develop a candidate summary based upon the knowledge, skills and abilities (KSA's) for the position. For example, if the position requires C#/SQL development experience along with the ability to gather software requirements, test, debug and train end users, outline your candidate's experience with these skills. If she has four of the five requirements, outline the four she does have. If she's missing one or even two, she may have other relevant experience. For example:

> *"While Susan doesn't have specific experience training end users, she has written technical documentation for end user reference and has made presentations to small and large groups."*

If she doesn't have any relevant experience with one of the skill areas, you may omit it from your summary and focus on the skills she does have. You may also provide a statement attesting to the candidate's ability or eagerness to learn a certain skill (given this is truly what you uncovered in the prescreen):

> *"While Susan doesn't have experience training end users, she was very articulate and communicated extremely well in our interview. In previous roles, she has comfortably worked with large and small groups. She is very excited about performing in a training capacity and is eager to discuss the company's training techniques and goals."*

Note for professional staffing firms: If you are presenting a candidate that has previously worked for your firm, include a statement about her performance! You don't have to be very detailed. A statement such as the following example will go a long way:

> *"Susan just recently completed a project for us and the client was extremely pleased with her software development skills and ability to meet tight deadlines."*

Her employment with your firm should also be included on the resume. Highlight this experience or make it stand out in a way that draws attention. **This not only eliminates a gap in employment, but also "advertises" your company.**

Similar information may be collected from references. **However, checking references takes time. Therefore, most recruiters don't do this until the candidate is further along in the process. However, if you've already checked references for a given candidate (this happens most often in external environments), include this information in the summary to help sell him!** If this is a new candidate and you need to get his information to the hiring manager ASAP, you should not wait on references. As stated earlier, **good candidates aren't on the market for very long. Do not wait for reference feedback before presenting a good candidate to the hiring manager.** You may collect the reference names and contact information, make the calls, but don't wait until they call you back unless your client or company requires this. If you do receive poor references after you've presented a candidate, let the hiring manager know about the information you've received. You don't have to be specific. Simply state that you wish to withdraw the candidate based upon the reference information you've received. Poor reference feedback doesn't happen often, but hiring managers will appreciate this information.

Providing major accomplishments of the candidate also makes an impact. For example:

> *"John developed and led the implementation of a major healthcare application, saving the company $2 million dollars in labor costs while increasing customer satisfaction by 15% due to faster and more accurate service."*

Sometimes, such information is on the resume. You don't have to repeat it if it's concise and stands out. **However, while most resumes are *sufficient*, they're not as marketable as they could be.** Therefore, gathering this information during the prescreen is very important. **Specific accomplishments and contributions to the bottom line make your candidates stand out from the rest.**

Once you have written your summary, you should review the resume and ensure it is appealing to the eye and free of errors. **This is more so the case for external recruiters because the resume represents your "product"—your candidate.** If the resume needs work, you should revise the formatting, correct errors or even rephrase content, but **you should never alter the content in a way that is misleading or false.** You may wish to point out the revisions to the candidate and ask him or her to revise it or you may have support staff that assists with this.

Editing resumes is a tedious process at times, but it's necessary in the external recruiting environment. You wouldn't make a business presentation with misspellings, grammatical errors or disorganized information. Resumes are no different! **In fact, sloppy resumes reflect poorly on the candidate, the recruiter and the firm. This can have lasting effects, so after the resume is cleaned up, proof it again!**

In internal environments, it is understood that candidates often apply online and there are hiring managers that will accept text resumes. However, they are often difficult to read and therefore, more time consuming for the hiring manager. In cases where you have a formatted resume, send it! If you don't have a formatted resume readily available, go ahead and send what you have. Let the hiring manager know you'll send a formatted resume as soon as you receive it from the candidate.

Notes for external recruiters:

- **You should always remove a candidate's contact information from the resume!** You don't want the client contacting your candidate directly. In some cases, you may even wish to remove the last name.

- **Always put your company logo on the resume or template** (see figure 6.1) so your client knows who submitted it. The client may have an interest in that candidate six months later and may not remember where it came from.

If you have several qualified candidates, it's recommended that you present your top three. You may submit more depending upon how many openings there are, but if there is only one opening, three is a good place to start. Once you get feedback from the hiring manager, it may be necessary to adjust your search and present more candidates. You may also learn that your hiring manager wishes that you continue sending candidates. Let your hiring manager guide you as to whether to spend more time on the search or if you hit the target with your first three.

After you have compiled your prescreen information and have a nice formatted resume, it's suggested that you use a template (similar to figure 6.1) for your presentation. Templates are professional, provide consistency and allow the hiring manager to easily find and refer to the information in which he or she is most interested. Templates should include your company name and logo at the top (even for internal recruiters) as this is more professional and further markets your brand. For external recruiters, this also let's the hiring manager know that the candidate came from your firm. This is especially helpful if a hiring manager is interested in the candidate six months later. He or she will know who to contact!

Figure 6.1: Sample Presentation Template

Candidate Profile		
Candidate Name:	**Position Referred For:**	**Availability:**
John Doe, JD, SPHR	Senior VP, Human Resources	January 8, 2007
Local Candidate:	**Compensation:**	**Other:**
No	$185,000	Desires 30% bonus

Background/Skills Summary

John is a results-driven **legal, human resources and operations executive** with a demonstrated success record of reducing operational and liability costs by up to $5 million dollars, while at the same time increasing organizational effectiveness through leadership, problem solving and change management. His experience includes **corporate litigation, employment law, labor relations, mergers & acquisitions, commercial transactions, risk management, establishment of operational procedures** and **managing multi-million dollar budgets.** Other skills include:

◆ Mediation	◆ Procurement	◆ Contract Negotiations
◆ Strategic Planning	◆ Program Management	◆ Information Systems
◆ New Program Development	◆ Policies & Procedures	◆ Financial Management

Resume

PROFESSIONAL EXPERIENCE
XYZ CORPORATION, New York,   1986–Present
Provides health care and human services to 25,000 clients locally, regionally and internationally with 1,600 employees and 65 sites in 10 states

VP, Support Services (2003–Present); VP, Human Resources (1997–2003); Director, Legal Services (1993–1997); Legal Counsel (1986–1993)
- Responsible for leading up to 100 associates and managing a $3–7 million budget
- Responsible for directing and achieving growth objectives for 10 departmental functions including legal, HR, MIS, purchasing, risk management, training and development, conference management services, office services and telecommunications
- Legal counsel for a broad spectrum of corporate and legal affairs to include investigation, negotiation, litigation and settlement of legal cases in the areas of business, employment, housing, construction, real estate, elder care, family, and corporate law matters, including mergers and acquisitions
- Internal legal consultant to all departments and locations including 530 health care beds & 2,200 housing units

EDUCATION
NEW YORK UNIVERSITY, New York City, NY
Juris Doctor
STANFORD UNIVERSITY, Stanford, CA
M.S. Industrial Relations; B.S. Business Administration

ADMISSIONS
- Member, State Bar of California
- Member, State Bar of New York

CERTIFICATIONS
SOCIETY OF HUMAN RESOURCE MANAGEMENT
- *Senior Professional in Human Resources (SPHR)*

Submittal Information

Contact Name: Recruiter X
Contact Information: 555-555-5555; recruiterx@mycompany.com
Date Submitted: 1/3/07

Once you've presented candidates, you should allow the hiring manager some time to review, but you should **be proactive in following up. If you've not heard from the hiring manager within 24–48 hours, follow up with him. Sometimes, you may need to follow up sooner. For example, if you know that your candidate has an offer from another company, follow up ASAP. If you're** working with an account manager, ensure that she knows the situation and that she follows up promptly. If you've developed different response times during the information gathering stage, use this as your rule of thumb for follow up. However, remember that 72 hours should be the maximum unless there are unavoidable circumstances (i.e., the hiring manager is out of town).

FORMAL INTERVIEWING & SELECTION METHODS

If the hiring manager is interested in speaking with the candidate(s) you presented, the formal interviewing phase begins. In the context of this book, formal interviewing is referred to as structured, face-to-face interviews. They are usually conducted by a key stakeholder other than the recruiter (e.g., the hiring manager) but recruiters may also formally interview candidates. It may be one interview with just the hiring manager or it may be with several interviewers, either as a group or individually. Interviewers may include the hiring manager, the recruiter, peers or other key managers. There may be a first round of interviews and if the candidate "passes", he or she is brought back for second or third round interviews. Second and third round interviews are often with individuals further up the "corporate ladder".

Attending interview sessions with the hiring manager, at least once, greatly benefits the recruiter. Recruiters may gain further knowledge of the interview process, the interviewer and the candidate. They may also obtain more details of the position or the company. All of this information enables the recruiter to work more collaboratively with the hiring manager. However, the hiring manager may not be comfortable with another person sitting in on his or her interview, so don't show up unexpectedly. If you wish to do this, obtain permission first. You may also wish to conduct your own formal interview in order to collaborate more thoroughly with the hiring manager with regard to the candidate's qualifications and competencies.

If a hiring manager is not interested in your candidate(s), find out why. This information allows you to refine your search and find better qualified candidates.

> Note for External Recruiters: Before your candidate interviews with your client, you should meet with him first (if you haven't already done so). Take this opportunity to provide detailed information about the company, environment, etc. and prepare him for the interview. Use this time to provide constructive feedback based upon your knowledge of the client. For example, he may need to dress differently, have more eye contact or he may need to emphasize his experience with "X".

> Ask him to call you after the client interview. If you don't hear from him, call him before the end of business the same day or the following morning. Find out if he's interested in the opportunity and if so, why. This will provide specific information about his motives and interests. Find out what kind of questions were asked of him so you may have a better understanding of what the client is seeking, allowing you to screen this information for future candidates. Get as much information as possible so you may prepare other candidates that may be interviewing with this client.

While the hiring manager is directly responsible for formally interviewing candidates, recruiters may also conduct such interviews and/or advise the hiring manager with regard to position competencies, types of interview questions to ask or interview structure.

Behavioral interviewing is a method often used when formally interviewing candidates because it uncovers behaviors that align with a position's key competencies. It's recommended that recruiters and hiring managers alike receive formal training in behavioral interviewing techniques. Behavioral interviewing requires structure, intuition, probing and interpretation.

Key points of behavioral interviewing are as follows:

• Behavioral Interview questions are based upon key competencies for a specific position.

- Behavioral interviewing is based on the premise that past behaviors are the best predictors of future behaviors.
- Behavioral interviewing, therefore, is not based upon what the candidate *would do* given a situation, but what he or she *has done* in a given situation.
- Candidates are asked to describe the situation, their actions and the result.
- Questions are not closed (yes or no answers) and require elaboration and thought on the part of the candidate.
- Interviewers use appropriate probing questions to extract needed information
- Behavioral interviewers should be formally trained in order to
  - determine the appropriate competencies
  - develop or select questions based upon those competencies
  - know when and how to probe
  - more accurately interpret answers
  - appropriately rate candidates

After the interviews have taken place, allow your hiring manager some time to assess the candidate(s). However, **use the same rule of thumb for follow up as for presenting resumes—within 24–48 hours** (unless you've established different response times in the information gathering stage). **You may need to follow up sooner given the candidate's status (i.e., if she has another offer). Discuss the interview with the hiring manager and determine what he liked or disliked about the candidate. Be sure to provide any feedback you may have based upon your prescreen or interview. If the hiring manager isn't interested, you should determine why. Understand the specific reason as this will help refine your search.** If the hiring manager does wish to move forward, there may be additional steps before an offer may be made:

- Professional references and/or work history verification
- Schedule second round of interviews
- Criminal background check
- Drug testing
- Skills testing
- Personality testing

Because some of the selection processes are likely outsourced, such as background/drug testing, or involves the expertise of a third party (i.e. a licensed psychologist to interpret personality assessments) recruiters are most often responsible for scheduling these and are not directly involved in performing them. Work history verification and reference checking, on the other hand, may fall under the responsibility of the recruiter or recruiter's support staff (in some cases, these services may also be outsourced).

Because professional reference checks and employment verification take time, many recruiters wait until the hiring manager shows interest before they invest their time in gathering this information. So if the hiring manager shows an interest, begin checking references and verifying employment as soon as possible. If you're having trouble reaching a reference, ask the candidate to contact him or her to help move things along. **Use a reference check form as a guideline to ensure you ask all the necessary questions.** Questions don't have to be asked in the exact order and follow-up questions may be necessary. Therefore, the word "guideline" is emphasized when using reference forms. **Keep in mind that references may be potential candidates if there are suitable openings. If you are an external recruiter, references may also be an opportunity for new business!** Sample reference questions are provided in figure 6.2.

> **Note for search firm recruiters:** The client may wish to perform the reference check. In some cases, you may be asked to obtain the reference information and forward it to HR or the hiring manager when it's completed.

Figure 6.2: Sample Reference Form

Candidate Name _____

Reference Name/Title _____
Company Name _____
Contact Information _____

Dates of Employment—From: _____ To:_____
Position(s) Held _____
Salary History _____
Reason for Leaving _____

1. Describe the candidate's job responsibilities as an employee of your company.

_____

_____

2. Describe his/her productivity and quality. Please provide specific examples.

_____

3. What were his/her strengths on the job? Weaknesses?

_____

_____

4. Describe his/her work attitude.

_____

5. How would you describe his/her relationships with others? Specifically, peers, immediate supervisor, other management and subordinates (if applicable)? Were there any individuals he/she didn't get along with? Explain.

_____

_____

_____

6. Did he/she have an issue with absenteeism or tardiness? Explain.

_____

7. Is this individual eligible for rehire? Why or why not?

_____

8. Other comments?

_____

_____

CHAPTER SEVEN

Stage 5: Offer

Recruiter's should have input as to who is hired and collaborate with the hiring manager after the selection process has been completed. However, the final decision to hire a candidate is up to the hiring manager (given the candidate satisfactorily meets all company requirements and selection criteria). Therefore, **the offer is set in motion after the selection process has been satisfactorily completed and the hiring manager has chosen a candidate. A verbal offer is recommended first in order to gauge the candidate's likelihood of acceptance. This is also an opportunity to discuss the key elements of the offer and prepare the candidate for what to expect in writing.** Keep in mind that there may be selection items that are completed after the verbal offer is made. For example, drug testing or criminal background checks are often completed after a verbal acceptance by the candidate. These can be very costly, so many companies wait until the candidate verbally accepts before completing them. The written offer should then have a statement indicating that the offer is contingent upon satisfactory results of these items.

Depending upon the company and environment, either recruiters or hiring managers may make the offer. **In the case of professional staffing or consulting firms, the recruiter should always make the offer as opposed to the client. This is because the candidate will be an employee of the recruiter's firm.** However, in cases involving a search firm, a client representative (hiring manager or HR professional) may wish to make the offer since the candidate will become the client's employee.

Offer Negotiations

Hiring managers may not always want to pay the candidate's desired compensation or in cases of professional staffing firms, the bill rate. When this happens, they usually want to lower the amount, but occasionally, they may be wowed by the candidate and want to offer more. This may be the case for star candidates who may have many opportunities. Offering more usually isn't an issue given it is justified and/or equitable, but offering less could be a problem. The candidate has expectations based upon previous discussions and what he believes he's worth. **While some candidates have unrealistic expectations, offering less to a star candidate may result in losing him altogether. An attempt to lowball a candidate just to save money or see if he'll accept is a grave mistake!** If a recruiter is concerned about the offer, it's important to discuss it with the hiring manager. Of course, this must be done professionally and as a partnership. The first step for the recruiter is to understand the hiring manager's reasoning for the proposed offer.

As mentioned in Chapter Four, it's important to understand your hiring manager's specific budget and expectations of the candidate up front to minimize unexpected (lower) offers at this stage. You may have performed your due diligence during the information gathering stage. You may have asked all the right questions and extracted all the needed information from your hiring manager. However, there is no fool proof way to prevent this every time and there may be viable reasons for this to occur, as follows:

1. The candidate may need specific skills training.
2. After interviewing, many weaknesses were uncovered and the candidate is not as strong as originally thought.
3. The responsibilities or the budget has changed since the position originally became available.
4. The hiring manager assumed a salary range based upon others' salaries, but this wasn't approved by upper management or HR.

This type of situation calls for negotiations with the candidate and hiring manager. This is often handled differently depending upon the environment in which you work.

External Offer Negotiations

If you are an external recruiter, you must balance your client's, candidate's and your firm's needs which can be a delicate process. **Don't back down immediately just because that's what your client wants. Instead, take a consultative approach by listening, understanding, explaining and advising.** You should listen to your hiring manager and understand why she wishes to lower the pay. However, you must represent your candidate (and your firm) fairly during this process. After hearing your hiring manager's reasoning, you should explain your own reasoning for the candidate's compensation (or bill rate in cases of professional staffing firms). Providing this type of supporting information will help the client understand the value of your original compensation or bill rate.

Some of the arguments may be as follows:

- The compensation or bill rate is the going market rate for professionals with similar KSA's in the industry.
- There's a lack of skilled candidates in the area (or even nationally).
- The client requires a hot skill which has a premium rate.
- The candidate may have other options and will likely decline anything less.

In addition to the above, professional staffing firms may have additional arguments for their bill rate. They may offer quality & retention incentives to their contract employees. These help ensure quality service and the assignment's completion. In other words, they're considered benefits for the client as well. Contract employees may receive additional benefits from the firm, which in turn, benefit the client by improving performance or by retaining employees. Some examples are provided below:

- Training
- Performance bonuses
- Healthcare benefits
- Paid vacation or personal time off
- Employee involvement programs
- Recognition awards

If any of the above (or others) is offered, make the hiring manager aware of this. Communicate the value of these and how it benefits her and her business. Of course, this must be handled tactfully and the recruiter must not push the issue. This is especially true in external environments. **Upsetting the client may result in losing the placement as well as future business!** This is a judgment call and in some cases, you may not be able to persuade the hiring manager in your direction.

If no compromises may be made with the hiring manager, you may approach the candidate and determine if he will accept lower pay (**for professional staffing firm recruiters, you determine pay—the client should only be negotiating a bill rate**). Discuss the information provided by the client and determine how firm the candidate is. You should attempt to sell the opportunity to him by outlining the entire package including the benefits, work environment, potential for advancement and learning opportunities. The candidate may be willing to accept the proposed offer and the verbal offer may then be made. If not, the hiring manager should understand the candidate's reasoning and situation in order to better understand his perspective. After careful discussions between recruiter and hiring manager, a compromise is usually made. There are rare circumstances when a compromise is not made and it may be back to the drawing board!

Professional staffing firms have another option to consider given there is no compromise from the candidate or the hiring manager. They may lower their bill rate and incur some (given the candidate is willing to incur some) or all of the loss. The recruiter should perform careful calculations to determine if lowering the bill rate is cost-effective for the firm. To review, the following is the gross profit example from Chapter One:

> *GP Example (Contract Employee):* A staffing firm bills their client $75/hr. and pays their contract employee $40/hr. for an assignment lasting approximately six months. The contract employee is eligible for and selects benefits. The fixed burden for contract employees receiving benefits is 23%. The GP per hour for this particular placement is calculated as follows:
>
> GP = $75 − $40 − ($40 x .23)
>
> GP = $35 − $9.20 = **$25.80/hr.**

If the hiring manager's bill rate is firm at $65/hr., the firm's GP on this place-ment decreases to $15.80/hr. The recruiter must determine if this is still prof-itable given the time, effort and costs put into the search as well as the potential for future business. The recruiter may very well decide that this is acceptable. Then again, he or she may not. It is a judgment call.

However, there may still be additional options. For example, while the candi-date may not be willing to take a $10/hr. pay cut, she may be willing to take a $5/hr. pay cut, thus sharing the loss. Another option concerns benefits. She may not really need benefits and if this can be negotiated, the burden decreases resulting in an increase in GP. As you can see, professional staffing firm recruiters have more variables to consider when negotiating a bill rate. To illus-trate how these variables may change, consider the following example:

> The candidate agrees to reduce her pay by $3 and she will also decline benefits. The burden for contract employees that don't receive benefits is 12%. The new GP is calculated below:
>
> GP = $65 – $37 – ($37 x .12)
>
> GP = $65 – $41.44 = **$23.56/hr.**

It's more acceptable to negotiate bill rates than it is to negotiate contingency fees. This is because bill rates vary per candidate and depends upon each can-didate's KSA's. **Search firms should never negotiate their contingency fee at the offer stage.** The contingency fee is established up front and an agreement is signed by both parties (or should be). If you lower your fee at this stage to make a placement, you may be expected to do this with each placement going forward! For this reason, the search firm only has two variables in which to negotiate. If the hiring manager wants to offer $90,000 instead of $100,000, the search firm still receives $27,000 in GP for this placement (given a 30% contin-gency fee). It is very well worth it to negotiate between the two parties and come to an offer acceptance in this case. The other option is starting the search all over again (given there are no other candidates). Therefore, the search firm recruiter must be an excellent negotiator in order to bring the two parties together and come to an agreement.

If and how you negotiate under these circumstances will be a judgment call. It will depend upon the time and effort you've put into the search, whether or not you may place the candidate somewhere else, the relationship you have with the client, and again, whether or not it is cost-effective for your firm.

Internal Offer Negotiations

Because internal recruiters work for the same company as the hiring manager, offer negotiations may not be as intense as it is in the external environment. However, hiring managers in these environments may also wish to adjust the compensation originally discussed. In this situation, **the internal recruiter should also understand the reasoning and discuss it more in-depth. The recruiter should then partner with the hiring manager and determine a fair offer. Information to be reviewed or considered includes the information obtained during the selection process, internal equity (what others in similar positions in the company are making with similar KSA's) and salary ranges provided by the compensation department.**

Like external recruiters, the internal recruiter must sell this offer to the candidate and ensure he understands the work environment, benefits, bonuses, incentives and opportunities. These provide a well-rounded picture of the offer than just base pay alone. If he still isn't willing to accept, further negotiations may take place. Again, you must understand his situation and perspective and determine what the motivations for declining are. Depending upon these motivations, there may be several options to consider in lieu of increasing the base pay. **For example, a hiring bonus, stock options, a flexible work schedule, etc. may also be considered in order to win over your candidate (this may be viable negotiations for the external recruiter as well).** If it is the base pay that's preventing him from accepting the offer, you must determine if this may be adjusted. This means you may have to consult with the hiring manager (and likely the HR Manager) one last time. You don't want to let a good candidate go, especially if it is a difficult position to fill or a position that requires a unique skill set.

Offer Declines

There are also times when a candidate may decline your offer for reasons beyond your control. For example, she may have a better offer in terms of compensation, opportunity or even commute time. If the reason does have to do with commute time or relocation, you may determine if telecommuting is acceptable for that specific position. In other words, not all reasons may be out of your control and you should think outside the box.

She may receive a counter offer from her current company that she just can't refuse. There are many reasons why a candidate SHOULD NOT accept counteroffers. A few of which are listed below:

- The company or supervisor may not forget the employee's desire to leave and hold this against him or her.
- The company may be making the counteroffer just to get rid of the employee on their own terms instead of the employee's terms.
- Companies may not come through with what they're offering. They may have good intentions (or they may not) and fully believe they will do what they say, but once the employee declines the outside offer, it just may not be as high a priority.
- Circumstances may change such as budgets, organizational structure, services, products, etc. and the company just simply can not keep their promises.

It is your job as the recruiter to understand the reason for the candidate's decline and present information she may not have considered. As mentioned, you may have to be creative in order to lure candidates, especially A players. If there are no inducements that will entice her, it may be back to the drawing board (hopefully, you have been proactive and have other candidates to interview). **It is very important that professional recruiters always recruit and keep an active flow of candidates. This is just one more example of why it's so important to be proactive.**

Offer negotiations aren't always necessary. Many times the offer aligns with what the candidate desires. Each situation may be different. However, once you receive a verbal acceptance, a written offer should then be provided (unless you're a professional search firm, in which case, all paperwork is likely the responsibility of the client). This written offer initiates the beginning of the onboarding stage.

CHAPTER EIGHT

Stage 6: Onboarding

Onboarding is the process of integrating new hires into the workforce. Effective onboarding programs will likely make a positive impression upon the new hire and provide the tools and information needed to be a success. Many people think of onboarding as just collecting a bunch of paperwork and while this is part of it, *effective* **onboarding should also include more meaningful information and direction.** While some of the onboarding process is unavoidably dull (e.g., paperwork and policy information), there are some things that may be done to actually capture the new hire's attention and make her excited to work there. **First and foremost, it's best to have a structured onboarding (also referred to as orientation) program that is allotted the appropriate amount of time.** In other words, don't show the new hire to his office, dump a bunch of paperwork on his desk and ask him to call you if he has any questions. This "sink or swim" attitude sends a message that neither you nor the company care about his success. Conversely, don't organize a full day of "information dump" where the employee can barely stay awake. **Companies must take the time to welcome new employees, make them feel valued and convey that the company does indeed care about their success** (Lee, 2005).

In figure 8.1 are some of the standard items included in a structured onboarding program. Note that human resources (which may include the recruiter) will usually conduct the orientation then transition new hires to their respective managers. Managers must also orient the new hire to the department, team and position. The topics with an asterisk next to them are items that should help the new hire become engaged and add more value.

Figure 8.1: Structured Orientation Outline

<u>Introduction</u>
- Icebreakers and introductions *
- Agenda
- Purpose and outcomes of orientation

<u>Company Information</u>
- History of the organization
- Products/services offered
- Markets
- Number of locations and employees
- Company Mission
- Company Vision
- Interesting facts, concepts, projects, ground-breaking achievements, etc.*
- Discuss how new hires will be able to contribute to the above *
- Organizational structure and/or organizational charts
- Key leaders introduce themselves to new hire(s) *

<u>HR Information</u>
- Company Culture
- Company Policies (dress code, sexual harassment, diversity, confidential information, ethical issues, etc.)
- Overview of benefits
- Emergency information
- Review of required paperwork and forms
- Provide specific contact information for different areas (i.e., payroll, benefits, grievances, etc.)

<u>Conclusion</u>
- Interactive games w/prizes to reinforce information (this may be integrated into different parts of the orientation) *
- Tour of the company *

- Questions
- Transition to Manager *

Departmental Orientation (conducted by the manager)
- Show new hire his/her workspace
- Team introductions & explanation of each person's role
- Departmental tour *
- Discuss departmental culture, how the manager will help him/her be successful, goals, action plans, expectations, etc. *
- Allow new hire to settle into his/her workspace
- Allow new hire to ask questions as needed
- Follow up with a lunch invitation to discuss goals, plans, etc. in greater detail *
- Begin mentoring, development and on-the-job training *

With all of this being said, recruiters' involvement in onboarding will differ depending upon the company and the environment in which they work. It will also depend upon the size and structure of the organization. For example, search firm recruiters will have little involvement in this process since the client onboards their own employees. Internal recruiters may be responsible for a portion of the onboarding process then transition it to the HR manager or generalist. Professional staffing and smaller consulting firm recruiters may be more heavily involved with onboarding since they may be the primary contact for HR issues. However, even when there is an HR manager within a company, recruiters may still be the ones responsible for, or at least assist with, the orientation session.

While the recruiters' specific role in onboarding may vary, one thing that they are responsible for is transitioning their candidate to the onboarding stage. After all, the recruiter has sourced and built a relationship throughout the recruitment process and have been the new hire's consistent connection to the organization. Recruiters must effectively wrap up any loose ends by collecting and/or turning over appropriate information and files, provide the new hire next steps and provide further direction to ensure this transition is seamless and smooth. This may even be true of search firm recruiters, although this transition is likely their only role with regard to onboarding. All other recruiters usually collect at least some of the paperwork required for employment as well. Some of the employment paperwork may include the application, resume, I-9 and W-4 forms and may even include the coordination of other items.

The form in figure 8.2 outlines some of the items that may be required for a new hire to be effectively onboarded. This type of checklist may be handled by someone other than the recruiter. Even if this is the case, it's important for recruiters to understand the items and transactions required during this stage to answer any additional questions and ensure the transition is smooth.

Figure 8.2

New Hire Checklist

Name_____

Department_____

Hire Date: _____

New Employee Paperwork
Responsibility: Human Resources
[ ] Application
[ ] Resume
[ ] W-4 and State Tax Forms
[ ] I-9
[ ] Reference information (must be completed by HR prior to starting work)
[ ] Benefits Summary
[ ] Health, Life & Disability Insurance Enrollment Forms
[ ] Signed Employee Handbook receipt form
[ ] Direct Deposit form
[ ] Explanation of pay procedures & time sheets (if used)
[ ] Completion of orientation training

System Logistics
Initiated by Manager; Responsibility: IT/Telecommunications Department
[ ] Computer System
[ ] Log-on ID
[ ] E-mail Account
[ ] Software installations, if applicable
[ ] Telephone System
[ ] Voice Mail

Other Logistics
Initiated by Manager; Responsibility: Administrative Assistant
[ ] Planner
[ ] Parking card
[ ] Security badge
[ ] Business cards
[ ] Credit card (must have approval from VP)
[ ] Keys (must have approval from VP)
[ ] Laptop (must have approval from VP)
[ ] Other: _____

Date Completed: _____

By: _____

Signed: _____

To be filed in employee's personnel file upon completion.

Structured onboarding is often associated with large corporations. However, it should be performed regardless of the organization's size. The items in figure 8.1 may even be more easily performed in smaller organizations and firms. For example, the professional staffing firm recruiter should not only introduce the new hire to key leadership (owner, president or branch manager), but he should be introduced to everyone in the office. Introduce him to the person that will be handling payroll and benefits, the account manager (if this is the staffing model) and so on. Provide a tour and show him where everyone sits and where the restrooms and break rooms are. Provide in-depth information about your company's culture, team, upcoming open-houses, events, rewards, newsletters, etc. Provide brochures, company history, company literature and organizational charts. **A structured and thoughtful onboarding approach is just as valuable to the employees of a small organization as it is for employees of a large corporation!** This is especially true in professional staffing (and sometimes smaller consulting) firms as it is important for your employees to feel connected to their *actual* employer (your firm). It is far too easy for them to begin their assignments and feel more like your clients' employees.

> **Note for professional staffing firm recruiters:** It's important that you follow up with your employee on the first day to ensure he made it to work, that everything is going smoothly and to offer any additional assistance that he may need. Once this follow up is made and every-thing is satisfactory, you may officially close the job order. There are rare circumstances when an employee will bail on you and not show up. This is rare, but it does occasionally happen. If you do have an instance where a contract employee doesn't show up, track him down immediately and ensure that the client knows of the steps you've taken to reach him. There may be a good excuse, for example, he may have had a fender bender on the way there. You don't want to assume the worst, but in the case that he just bailed on you and your client, work to rectify it immediately. The client will likely be upset over the matter and the best way to resolve it is to find someone else, if the client's agreeable to this (which is yet another reason why you should always proactively recruit). It also doesn't hurt if you (or the account man-ager) invite the hiring manager to lunch or make an in-person visit to apologize for the situation.

CHAPTER NINE

Stage 7: Retention

Retention is an effort to keep talented employees within the organization. But whose responsibility is it? Is it the recruiter's? Is it the HR manager's or the organization's leadership? In most cases, it's all of the above. Most often, **retention initiatives are the responsibility of human resources as far as designing programs or training the organization's leadership** (managers and executives at all levels). For example, career planning is a type of retention program because it promotes employees' career advancement within the company. Other benefits, such as on-site daycare, may retain the employee that wants to spend more time with his children. Cross training may allow an employee to develop new skills, not to mention, a change of pace. This makes the work more interesting and therefore, assists in employee retention. HR may also provide coaching or training programs to management so they may learn how to better "connect with their employees" (Stevens-Huffman, 2006 ¶ 14). The organization's **leadership may play the most vital role in retention since they are directly managing, leading and interacting with employees on a daily basis. How they lead, mentor, develop and treat their employees may have the biggest impact when it comes to employee retention** (Stevens-Huffman, 2006).

While HR and leaders are most often associated with retention, recruiters do contribute either directly or indirectly to these efforts. Hiring quality employees in and of itself directly contributes to retention. Conversely, poor quality only creates turnover. Whether the turnover rate is high or low, it will have a direct impact on recruiting. If the turnover is low, recruiters have fewer backfill positions and may concentrate on strategy and/or newly created positions. If the turnover rate is high, recruiters will spend an enormous amount of time backfilling the same positions. Because retention directly affects recruiting, **high performance recruiters consider retention as a component of their recruiting strategy.** For example, recruiters may start by "first identifying which source(s) have the lowest turnover rates (generally referrals) and developing a plan to identify mission-critical positions and key individuals where turnover would significantly hurt the firm. Next identify the reasons why top performers stay and leave your firm. Resolve those issues." (Sullivan, 2006, ¶ 10).

Having a quality recruiting and onboarding program also plays a role in retention. **Ensuring quality and service throughout the recruitment lifecycle will no doubt make a good first impression and set a positive tone for the new hire. Conversely, poorly structured and service oriented recruitment processes will leave a bad impression and may leave the new hire thinking twice about accepting the position.** A quality-related item that recruiters are directly responsible for is the new hire survey. These are usually sent within a month of the new hire's employment to ensure she's had a pleasant experience during the recruiting, onboarding and new hire processes. This not only helps improve the recruiting system, but it also gauges the employee's attitude and satisfaction with her employment thus far. This information is a strong indicator of whether or not she's a flight risk and allows management to address these issues before it's too late. **Simply communicating with new hires during the first months of employment is extremely important to their retention.**

Other recruiters (except search firm recruiters) may contribute to retention efforts by participating in HR or company sponsored projects regarding new benefits, cultural changes, employee involvement, employee development or career coaching, to name a few. Recruiters have valuable insight when it comes to employees' needs and motivations. After all, recruiters are directly responsible for bringing these employees into the organization and have developed relationships with them.

Recruiters in professional staffing firms (as a whole) are generally more involved in individual retention efforts than are recruiters in other environments. If they're not, they should be! This is because the **recruiter becomes the contract employee's "agent" (so to speak). The recruiter must ensure that the** contract employee completes his current assignment and is retained for future assignments. Therefore, the recruiter must keep in close contact with him and further develop the relationship. The recruiter must plan ahead and determine clients that may utilize his KSA's. This must be done prior to the contract employee's end date (at least a month) to ensure retention. If not, he may become an employee of a competing firm or unemployed. Because contract employees are the livelihood of the firm, the bottom line is negatively affected when they're not retained. Recruiters' compensation is also negatively affected, so they must be extremely involved and motivated when it comes to retention.

Also, because the contract employee works at the client's site, it's easy for him to become disconnected from his actual employer—the firm. The recruiter must bridge this gap by engaging him in company events, referral programs (current employees are the best source for referrals!), employee reward programs, addressing benefit or payroll issues, attendance, performance or issues in general concerning the client. The recruiter may visit the contract employee at the client's site, call him on a consistent basis or take him to lunch to ensure everything is going smoothly and to address any issues or concerns. Developing a relationship with your employee will not only keep him connected to you and your firm, but will build loyalty and trust. He'll be more likely to communicate those positions your competition is contacting him about so you may thwart these efforts. He may even provide enough information that you may follow up on these openings yourself. He is also more likely to communicate an issue concerning his assignment so you may resolve it before it gets out of hand. Therefore, **the recruiter's relationship with the contract employee is a major factor with regard to retention.**

Keep in mind that the goal of retention is to retain and effectively utilize talent. Therefore, **the professional staffing firm recruiter must verify performance** and be creative if another position isn't readily available. Some firms may allow the contract employee to work on internal projects until he is placed. Others may provide computer based training (a benefit many of these firms provide) during the interim. Still, some may ask the contract employee to assist with an open house or present at a client event in order to keep him engaged with the firm.

Search firm recruiters, on the other hand, are less involved when it comes to retention as their placement (the new hire) is the responsibility of their client (the employer). However, search firm recruiters still play some role in retention. As mentioned previously, hiring quality employees is considered a retention effort. Search firm recruiters may also have a period in which they guarantee their placement. This may be one month, three months or up to six months. The recruiter doesn't want to perform the search all over again, so he or she is very motivated to ensure the placement stays put. In these cases, the recruiter may make informal calls to ensure the placement's job satisfaction and intent to stay. However, the recruiter must be very careful in doing this. Clients are very protective of their employees when it comes to search firms (as they should be) and you don't want your client to think you're trying to solicit an employee for another client. Because of this, search firm recruiters may opt to contact their placements when they're at home.

Whatever the environment, talent **retention is a business goal of any company and high performance recruiters align their efforts with this goal in mind.** Even search firm recruiters must make retention a goal or else they'll lose business. There aren't many clients that will continue paying a large fee if the search firm isn't able to place employees that stay. To conclude, consider the following statements by Dr. John Sullivan (2006, ¶ 10):

> "If you don't currently 'own' retention, seize it now. Remember that if retention is ignored or done poorly, it has a dramatic impact on recruiting. Without focusing on retention, the recruiting function will have to work twice as hard to fill the vacancies that result from high turnover rates. High turnover rates will also damage your external image and make recruiting new top performers much more difficult."

CHAPTER TEN

Stage 8: Measurement & Quality Assurance

Measurement and quality assurance is a means to evaluate, analyze and improve recruitment systems in order to achieve desired company and recruiting goals. Perhaps you've heard or have said the following:

> "I'm extremely busy just trying to perform my recruitment activities. Why do I need to spend time measuring aspects of my work?" There are several answers to this question!

- To determine if you're achieving desired results and goals
- To improve hiring practices, efficiency, effectiveness and quality
- To determine cost effectiveness
- To determine stakeholders' satisfaction (managers, applicants, candidates, new hires and company executives)
- To make effective decisions
- To be competitive!

As mentioned in earlier chapters, recruiting has become a valued component of the organization and if you're a third party (external) recruiter, recruiting is the direct service and livelihood of your organization! Also mentioned in earlier chapters, the competition is fierce among recruitment firms and even fiercer when it comes to competing for individual talent. **Using recruitment data and information to improve performance, effectiveness and efficiency** will no doubt give you a competitive edge in what some have termed "The War for Talent".

There are many measurements that companies use to measure their recruiting programs. In a nutshell, there are four basic categories of recruiting metrics as follows:

- New Hire Quality—assessing initial quality and performance of new hires
- Customer Satisfaction—assessing managers', new hires' and candidates' satisfaction with the recruiter's service and hiring practices
- Time—assessing the time it takes for a recruiter to complete the stages within the recruiting lifecycle as well as the entire time taken to fill a position
- Cost—associated with staffing activities, tools and resources

New Hire Quality

New hire quality is considered the most important metric in recruiting. After all, it doesn't matter how fast or how service oriented you are if you're not placing the right people. **Placing poor quality candidates actually costs the company money.** The best way to assess new hire quality is to first develop the criteria for quality in partnership with the hiring manager. After the criteria are determined, a survey should be developed using a point scale in order to quantify the results. Areas for comments should also be included in order to qualify information and understand reasoning behind the ratings. The survey should be sent to the hiring manager within three to six months of employment. This amount of time is recommended as this allows new hires to learn their role and adapt to their new work environment, giving hiring managers a better assessment of overall quality.

Other long term efforts to track new hire quality include a review of formal performance evaluations, promotional information and retention (Staffing.org, 2006). This type of information takes more effort and time to measure, but may be tracked through a company's HRIS (human resource information system).

Customer Satisfaction

For recruiters, there are at least two customers: the hiring manager and the new hire (candidates not hired may also be considered customers). The hiring manager's "satisfaction criteria" should be established up front so the recruiter understands the expectations (Staffing.org, 2006). As mentioned in Chapter Four, it's best to do this during the information gathering stage. At this stage, key measurements such as quality of candidates, expected time to fill or time to start, recruiter follow up and response time, etc. should be established (these are not all inclusive and may vary depending upon the hiring manager). Recruiters should evaluate themselves throughout the lifecycle rather than waiting until the position is filled. After the position is filled, a survey based upon the key measurements or other satisfaction criteria (see Chapter Four, figure 4.1, "key measurements") should be sent to the hiring manager to determine his or her level of satisfaction.

New hires are also customers and should be considered as a component of this metric (Staffing.org, 2006). In assessing new hire satisfaction, it is important for recruiters to understand what defines exceptional service for the new hire. Based upon this, a survey should be developed for new hires to complete. Some recruiter-related items to consider for new hire satisfaction include:

- Response time
- Knowledge of the position
- Knowledge of the company
- Information shared
- Effective selection criteria
- Effective coordinating/scheduling
- Effective interpersonal communications
- Professionalism

Similar questions regarding the hiring manager and other hiring practices should also be considered as this provides a well-rounded picture of the new hire's experience. Again, each of these surveys should be on a point scale to easily quantify the results with room for comments in order to qualify the results.

Providing similar surveys to all candidates (not just the ones selected) will also provide invaluable information regarding your recruiting performance (Staffing.org, 2006). While this takes more time and response rates may be low, this information may help you improve your operations and send the message that your company cares about its quality of service at all levels.

Time

Time refers to how long it takes from the date recruiting is initiated to move from one recruiting stage to another and ultimately, for the employee to start work. The contracted time to start "is the number of days between the date that recruiting is initiated and the date the recruiter and hiring manager mutually agree that the position will be filled" (Staffing.org, 2006, p. 17). The contracted time to start should meet the following criteria:

- Be determined up front, preferably before actual recruiting begins
- Be determined in partnership with the hiring manager
- Be agreed upon by both parties
- Be documented in terms of a specific date (this means that "ASAP", "soon", "yesterday" and "no hurry" don't count)
- Be reasonable given the type of position, market and business need, among others

Once the hiring manager and recruiter have an agreed upon contracted time to start, the actual time to start is measured against this. This is similar to how projects are estimated and reflects the recruiter as a partner as opposed to an order taker. Keep in mind that this "contracted time may be changed upon mutual consent of the hiring manager and the recruiter. This allows for what are sometimes inevitable changes in priorities or availability that adversely impact the hiring process" (Staffing.org, 2006, p. 17).

Actual vs. contracted time to start is a more valuable metric than simply measuring "days to start". As a stand-alone metric, the number of days for an employee to start work doesn't provide a whole lot of meaning to stakehold-ers. Consider the following comparison:

Recruiter A's metric for "days to start" is 140 days

Recruiter B's metric for "actual vs. contracted time to start" is 90:100 or -10 days (ten days prior to the contracted time to start).

Which one provides the most information? For **Recruiter A**, does 140 days mean anything? Is the recruiter performing well, average or poor? What if Recruiter A is recruiting executives? Then this would be an exceptional metric given the quality is high! What if these were entry level sales positions? Then maybe this metric isn't so good. Many companies average the days to start for each recruiter's filled positions. Suppose these are a vast array of positions, including entry level professionals to highly skilled and middle management positions? This metric then becomes even more ambiguous. It's unclear exactly how the recruiter is performing with regard to time.

Now, what about **Recruiter B**? What could be immediately determined from this is that the recruiter and hiring manager have formed a partnership by determining a contracted time to start and the recruiter holds herself accountable for meeting or exceeding this goal. **More importantly, this metric shows that the recruiter has exceeded expectations by placing the employee ten days prior to the contracted time.** You may also average actual vs. contracted to time start for each recruiter's filled positions. Unlike days to start, this averaged metric does provide relevant meaning. For example:

The recruiter fills three positions. The first is three days prior (-3) to the contracted time to start, the second is ten days after (+10) and the third is thirteen days prior (-13). The average is calculated by adding each and dividing it by the total number of positions, as follows:

Average "actual vs. contracted time to start" = $(-3 + 10 + -13)/3$

$$-6/3 = -2$$

This means that the recruiter is exceeding the contracted time to start projection, on average, by two days. A positive number would indicate that the recruiter is going beyond the contracted time start date and not meeting the time expectations.

While "actual vs. contracted time to start" is the primary time metric, there are similar incremental metrics that may be useful. Measuring actual vs. contracted time in incremental stages may provide some information as to how the recruiter is handling each stage and may provide some insight for improvement. This is especially true if the recruiter is not meeting the contracted time to start goal. Reviewing the incremental time frames may help target the problem areas and more importantly, resolve them. For example, if the recruiter exceeded the time frame for completing first interviews, was this because the hiring manager delayed? Did the recruiter delay? Did the recruiter understand the position requirements? If any of these were the case, perhaps the information gathering stage wasn't conducted properly. Perhaps the recruiter didn't gather thorough information or didn't establish response times. Also, the timeframes may have needed adjustment due to unforeseeable business circumstances. Once the specific problem(s) is identified, the recruiter may correct these issues for future searches and improve upon his or her actual vs. contracted time to start metric.

Cost

Cost per hire (CpH) is probably the most popular metric associated with recruiting costs. This is calculated by taking the recruiting costs and dividing it by the number of positions filled as shown below:

$$CpH = Recruiting\ Costs/Number\ of\ Positions\ Filled$$

The CpH calculation inherently assumes that all positions are equal and relies on the total number of positions filled as an indicator of productivity. For this reason, **cost per hire can be misleading.** For example, it doesn't address the fact that higher level positions cost more to fill than lower level positions. Volume recruiting, for example, 100 customer service positions in a call center, may cost about the same as recruiting one CEO. It also doesn't address geographical, functional or industry differences in positions and therefore, cost per hire figures are ambiguous, providing little meaning without further investigation (Staffing.org, 2006).

The Recruiting cost ratio (RCR) was developed by Staffing.org (www.staffing.org) and addresses these inherent problems with the cost per hire calculation. **RCR provides a better picture of recruiting efficiency** because it takes into account the actual compensation of each external hire. The formula is provided below:

RCR = (Total Staffing Costs/Total Compensation Recruited) x 100

"When multiplied by 100, the result yields a percentage. A lower percentage denotes a more efficient recruiting function" (Staffing.org, 2006, p. 21).

Total staffing costs are calculated by summing four recruiting categories:

- Internal expenses (fixed operating expenses, e.g., recruiter's salaries, recruitment technologies, etc.)
- External expenses (sourcing costs, e.g., advertising, referral bonuses, etc.)
- Signing bonuses
- Travel, relocation and Visa expenses

The total compensation recruited is calculated by adding first-year base salaries for all external hires. Therefore, internal hires are not included in this calculation (Staffing.org, 2006, pp. 22–23).

Because sourcing is a cost that can be controlled, it's important to track costs of individual sources as well as the hires that come from each. For example, if you're spending $10,000 a year on an internet job board, yet you have no hires from this site, you may want to consider a more effective source! The quality of hires from the source must also be considered.

As mentioned previously, external recruiters must measure the gross profit for each of their placements and determine the overall GP they contribute to the firm's bottom line.

Final Notes

When determining the metrics and tools to utilize for your recruiting program, remember that they should align with business goals. The four categories of metrics outlined in this chapter measure new hire quality, quality of recruiting service, cost-effectiveness and time, which are critical to a company's perform-ance, revenue, cost savings and retention. There are other metrics that are in existence that may or may not be useful and you must thoroughly assess which ones actually produce valuable and useful information. For example, a common misconception is that the ratio of positions open to positions filled is a metric of efficiency. Wrong! This provides no relevant information as there are many underlying factors as to why positions are open or filled.

Another metric that is used widely and thought to portray productivity are measurements related to volume. Companies often quantify how many candidates were contacted, prescreened, referred to the hiring manager, interviewed, made an offer, accepted or declined the offer and lastly, how many positions were filled (candidates started work). Some companies even have quotas based upon these. This is a huge mistake! **Interpreting volume alone as an indicator of productivity is not only misleading, but counter productive! These types of metrics force recruiters to focus on quantity rather than quality, resulting in recruiters prescreening, interviewing, etc. just to boost their numbers. Filling seats for the sake of quotas costs the company time and money due to poor hires.**

However, like incremental time metrics, volume measurements may serve some purpose in flagging recruitment bottle necks or problem areas. This could then be investigated and the recruiter may improve their performance or other components of the program (i.e. technology). For example, if the recruiter prescreened 20 candidates but didn't refer any to the hiring manager, this may be a problem. Perhaps she's selecting the wrong candidates to prescreen in the first place or she's being too selective during the prescreen. She may also be dropping the ball when it comes to referring candidates to the hiring manager. So while there may be some usefulness in all metrics, they must be used for the appropriate purpose and other factors may need to be considered in order to extract relevant meaning.

One thing that's certain is that if you have no metrics, you have no way to accurately gauge or improve performance. If you use the wrong metrics, you may be counterproductive. You must assess the appropriate metrics to show performance and contributions to the bottom line, fully implement them and consistently track and evaluate the data. Don't be afraid to make adjustments to your metrics or experiment with new metrics. Involve everyone in the program with this process and ensure the value of measurement and continuous improvement is understood and supported. Following these tips will assist in developing high performance recruiters and high performance recruiting programs. For more information on staffing and human resource metrics, see www.staffing.org and www.humanresourcemetrics.org.

CHAPTER ELEVEN

Conclusion

As mentioned in the introduction, recruiting is more complex than one might think. It consists of selling, project management, consulting, advising, negotiating, persuasion, research and human resource management. The points touched upon here are just the tip of the iceberg as complete textbooks have been written on interviewing, employment law, selling, negotiation and human resources, among others. This reading hits on the high points for high performance recruiting and gives you an inside roadmap to success.

To conclude, listed below are tips and best practices for quick reference and key development areas. The information provided in bold throughout this book should also serve as quick reference as you begin or continue your recruiting career. Dr. John Sullivan (2002) also provides some very useful information and tips in his article, *Are You a "World-Class" Recruiter?* The specific link may be found in the References section of this book.

- **Use technology and other resources to the fullest to minimize administrative transactions and paper shuffling;** set up search agents to mine databases for you or set up prescreen questionnaires to assist in narrowing down the pool of candidates.

- Approach recruitment as a project—**strategize, organize, execute and measure.**

- **Set weekly, monthly, quarterly and yearly goals that align with business goals;** continually measure your progress and accomplishments and realize that you may need to adjust these goals as the market, industry, talent pool or competition changes.

- **Keep up with industry trends and the profession;** read books and articles, join recruiting or HR organizations and evaluate what your competition is doing.
- Do more than just source. **Partner, consult, sell, advise, negotiate and manage relationships!**
- Always document key information in your database to **effectively manage your candidates, jobs and activities.** Keep open communications with others on your recruiting team.
- Always **research the company and department in which you're conducting a search**; get as much information about company/department culture, organizational structure, number of employees, products/services offered, internal operations, etc. Research on the web as well!
- **Always source and ask for referrals for "hot skills" even when you don't have a specific position in mind.** Be proactive!
- **Develop creative and attention-grabbing job postings;** copying and pasting a job description is less likely to hold your readers' attention!
- **Always evaluate and uncover potential opportunities when speaking with professional references.** These may be new business for the third party recruiter or potential candidates for any recruiter!
- **Network** in organizations, conferences, seminars, etc. where you may learn about the industry in which you recruit (for example, healthcare) and meet potential candidates.
- Always **search your own database, networks and referrals first.**
- **Recognize talent** that you may already have within your workforce.
- **Offer referral bonuses!** This is a great motivator and is most often well worth the expense!
- When interviewing, **listen and apply the 80/20 rule;** allow your candidates to do 80% of the talking, but ensure they stay on track!
- Ask candidates where they've interviewed or where they're currently interviewing so you may **understand where he or she is in the process. For external recruiters, these are also business leads!**
- **Provide your candidates constructive feedback** so they may improve upon their resume, interviewing skills, appearance, communications,

etc. Be tactful and deliver messages in a way that lets them know you're looking out for them.

- Always **ensure legal compliance** throughout the recruiting lifecycle. Do not base submission, interview or hiring decisions on criteria that has nothing to do with the position!
- Follow up after submissions and client interviews within 48 hours, preferably 24 hours. **Don't wait for the hiring manager to call you a week later.** Your candidate may find another job while you're waiting!
- Create top five or top ten lists of your star candidates and stay in touch with them! **Be proactive in marketing them to your hiring managers.**
- Service, Service, Service! **Be professional, responsive and provide exceptional customer service to <u>everyone</u>.**
- **Make quality of hires your priority** as opposed to quantity of hires.
- **Measure retention** by determining how long your hires are staying with the company. This is an indicator of your success!
- **If candidates are declining, find out why!** Sell the position and negotiate between candidate and hiring manager to **prevent star candidates from getting away.**
- **Anticipate needs in advance** (workforce planning). Again, you must be proactive!
- Help build your company's image and brand! **There's more to sell than just the position itself.**
- **Be strategic and develop new recruitment strategies or programs** that may help you or your company become more successful.
- **Prioritize** your most critical positions!
- **Continually learn!**
- **Advise and partner** with hiring managers throughout the recruiting lifecycle.
- **Take on challenging positions or projects** in order to improve your performance.
- **Share your talents and mentor others!**

APPENDIX

Helpful Websites:

www.6figurejobs.com
Job board focusing on six figure positions and candidates

www.americanstaffing.net
American Staffing Association

www.blr.com
Business and legal reports

www.bls.gov/oco
Occupational outlook handbook

www.careerbuilder.com
General job board

www.dice.com
IT job board

www.diversityinc.com
Site devoted to diversity articles, resources and tools

www.erexchange.com
Electronic Recruiting Exchange—recruiting resources, blogs, guides, etc.

www.findlaw.com
Legal search engines and links, including employment law

www.homefair.com
Relocation information

www.hoovers.com
Business and company research

www.hotjobs.com
General job board

www.hr.com
Human resource site with articles, trends, tools, etc.

www.hreonline.com
Human resource executive online—strategic HR information, articles & resources

www.hrmguide.com
Network of linked HR websites containing hundreds of HR Management-related articles, features and links.

www.hrps.org
Human Resource Planning Society

www.humanresourcemetrics.org
Site dedicated to HR measurements and scorecards

www.ipma-hr.com
International Public Management Association for HR

www.linkedin.com
Online network

www.monster.com
General job board

www.nicheboards.com
Niche job boards—multiple sites specializing in niche professions

www.recruitersalliance.com
Pay-for service site specializing in job orders and candidate splits

www.recruiterlife.com
Recruiting website

www.recruitersnetwork.com
Recruiting articles, trends, tools, resources, best practices, etc.

www.ryze.com
Online network

www.salary.com
Salary data, reports, surveys

www.shrm.org
Society for Human Resource Management (SHRM)

www.staffing.org
Staffing metrics, performance, tools and resources

www.weddles.com
Resources for employment, personal development and career success

www.wetfeet.com
Company research, insider guides, references

www.workforce.com
Human Resources and business-related articles

www.worldatwork.com
Compensation and benefits

REFERENCES

Lee, D. (2005, November 22). How to Avoid the Four Deadliest Onboarding Mistakes. *Electronic Recruiting Exchange.* Retrieved October 12, 2006 from http://www.ere.net/articles/db/3F9DEDC4BD074E23A72AD98B938382CA.asp

Recruit. In M. Agnes (Ed.), *Webster's New World Dictionary, Pocket Books Paperback Edition* (p. 539, 4th ed.). (2003). New York: Wiley Publishing

Recruiters Network (1997–2007). Boolean Operators. Retrieved July 28, 2006, from Recruiters Network web site: http://www.recruitersnetwork.com/resources/boolean.htm

Staffing.org (1998–2007). Recruitment Metrics. Retrieved November 17, 2006, from Staffing.org web site: http://www.staffing.org/staffinga-z/info/Measurement/Recruitment%20Metrics/

Staffing.org., Inc. (2006, October) *Staffing Metrics Toolkit* (version 4). Willow Grove, Pennsylvania.

Staffing.org., Inc. (2004). *101 Established Recruiting Processes.* [Electronic Document]. Willow Grove, Pennsylvania.

Stevens-Huffman, L. (2006, July). Talent Retention Becomes a Recruiting Strategy. *Workforce.com.* Retrieved December 20, 2006, from http://www.workforce.com/archive/feature/24/44/58/index.php?ht=retention%20and%20recruiting%20retention%20and%20recruiting

Sullivan, J. (2006, January). Why Not Do Something Strategic in Recruiting? Electronic Recruiting Exchange. Retrieved January 5, 2007, from http://www.ere.net/articles/db/6CE921F36B394255801745D201F8158C.asp

Sullivan, J. (2002, March 4). Are You a "World-Class" Recruiter? *Electronic Recruiting Exchange.* Retrieved August 23, 2006, from http://www.ere.net/articles/db/F3D1AA2B6B0047648E4401919E92E173.asp/

Sullivan, J. (2002, November). Why You Need Workforce Planning. *Workforce.com.* Retrieved November 8, 2006, from http://www.workforce.com/section/00/feature/23/35/44/index.html

Illegal Interview Questions (2001, January). *USATODAY.com.* Retrieved January, 9, 2007, from http://www.usatoday.com/careers/resources/interviewillegal.htm.

Weddle, P. (2003, August). A Job Ad For the Ages. *Recruiters Network.* Retrieved October 23, 2006, from http://www.recruitersnetwork.com/articles/article.cfm?ID=1035

Workforce Planning—Who Does What? (2002, October). *Workforce.com.* Retrieved November 8, 2006, from http://www.workforce.com/archive/article/23/34/05.php?ht=%22workforce%20planning%22%20%22workforce%20planning%22

978-0-595-42781-9
0-595-42781-2